RYA
YACHTMASTER SCHEME
INSTRUCTOR HANDBOOK

© RYA
First published 1990, revised edition 2004
This edition 2015
Reprinted October 2016, November 2017,
October 2018
The Royal Yachting Association
RYA House, Ensign Way,
Hamble, Southampton,
Hampshire SO31 4YA

Tel: 02380 604 100

Web: www.rya.org.uk
Follow us on Twitter @RYAPublications or
on YouTube

We welcome feedback on our publications at
publications@rya.org.uk

You can check content updates for RYA
publications at www.rya.org.uk/go/bookschangelog

ISBN 978-1-910017012
RYA Order Code G27

Cover design: *Pete Galvin*
Illustrations: *Hamble School of Yachting, Doug Innes,
Andrew Norton, Powerboat Training UK,
sportscotland National Centre Cumbrae*
Typeset: *HL Studios*
Printed in China through World Print Ltd.

Sustainable
Forests

CONTENTS

INTRODUCTION

The RYA Yachtmaster Scheme is aimed at encouraging high standards of seamanship and navigation skills in those who go to sea in either sailing boats or motor vessels. Whether your students' interests are in boating for fun or in gaining skills and qualifications for a career at sea in small commercial vessels, the range of courses has something for everyone.

The scheme has been in operation since the early 1970s and has been so successful that various qualifications contained within it have been selected by UK regulators and those of other countries as the qualifications of choice for commercial applications, as well as leisure.

The strength and success of this training scheme lies with the skills and integrity of the many thousands of instructors and examiners who train and assess within it. The guidance provided within this book is intended to assist instructors and examiners in ensuring they do all they can to meet the high standards expected of them, not only by the RYA but also by the students they will be teaching and appraising. The different instructional and coaching techniques have been fine-tuned through decades of experience and feedback from thousands of experienced trainers and students. I am confident that you will benefit from their experience.

I hope you enjoy your instructor course and wish you every success in working within the RYA Yachtmaster Scheme.

Richard Falk
Director of Training & Qualifications

1 RYA INSTRUCTOR CODE OF CONDUCT FOR RYA INSTRUCTORS, COACH ASSESSORS, TRAINERS AND EXAMINERS

This document outlines the code of conduct under which all holders of RYA Instructor qualifications and RYA training appointments (hereafter referred to as Instructors) are required to comply. The code of conduct is intended to make clear to all participants, Instructors and RYA appointment holders the high standards to which all are expected to conform. Instructors must:

► If working with people under the age of 18, read and understand the Child Protection Policy as detailed on the RYA website at www.rya.org.uk.

► Respect the rights, dignity and worth of every person and treat everyone equally within the context of their sport.

► Place the well-being and safety of the student above the development of performance or delivery of training. They should follow all guidelines laid down by the RYA and hold appropriate insurance cover either individually or through the RYA-recognised training centre in which they are working.

▶ Not develop inappropriate working relationships with students (especially children). Relationships must be based on mutual trust and respect and not exert undue influence to obtain personal benefit or reward.

▶ Encourage and guide students to accept responsibility for their own behaviour and performance.

▶ Hold relevant, up to date, and governing body qualifications, as approved by the RYA.

▶ Ensure that the activities they direct or advocate are appropriate for the age, maturity, experience and ability of the individual.

▶ At the outset, clarify with students (and where appropriate their parents) exactly what is expected of them and what they are entitled to expect.

▶ Always promote the positive aspects of the sport (e.g. courtesy to other water users).

▶ Consistently display high standards of behaviour and appearance.

▶ Not do or neglect to do anything which may bring the RYA into disrepute.

▶ Act with integrity in all customer and business to business dealings pertaining to RYA training.

▶ Not teach RYA courses outside of the framework of RYA-recognised training centres.

▶ Notify the RYA immediately of any court imposed sanction that precludes the Instructor from contact with specific user groups (for example children and vulnerable adults).

2 RYA EQUALITY POLICY

2.1 OBJECTIVES

► To make boating an activity that is genuinely open to anyone who wishes to take part.

► To provide the framework for everyone to enjoy the sport, in whatever capacity and to whatever level the individual desires.

► To ensure that the RYA's services, including training schemes, are accessible to all, including those who have been under-represented in the past.

2.2 POLICY STATEMENT

The Royal Yachting Association is committed to the principle of equality of opportunity and aims to ensure that all present and potential participants, members, Instructors, coaches, competitors, officials, volunteers and employees are treated fairly and on an equal basis, irrespective of sex, age, disability, race, religion or belief, sexual orientation, pregnancy and maternity, marriage and civil partnership, gender reassignment or social status.

2.3 IMPLEMENTATION

▶ The RYA encourages its affiliated clubs and organisations and its recognised training centres to adopt a similar policy, so that they are seen as friendly, welcoming and open to all.

▶ Appointments to voluntary or paid positions with the RYA will be made on the basis of an individual's knowledge, skills and experience and the competences required for the role.

▶ The RYA will relax regulations in relation to RYA training schemes which may inhibit the performance of candidates with special needs, provided that the standard, quality and integrity of schemes and assessments are not compromised.

▶ The RYA reserves the right to discipline any of its members or employees who practise any form of discrimination in breach of this policy.

The effectiveness of this policy will be monitored and evaluated on an ongoing basis.

3 RYA ORGANISATION

RYA Yachtmaster Scheme courses may only be run at an RYA-recognised training centre. For details on how to become recognised, please contact the RYA Training Department.

Centres fall into three main categories:

▶ Commercial centres which are open to the public

▶ Clubs that provide training to their members

▶ Restricted organisations such as the Armed Forces or the Police Force.

Recognition is vested in the Principal who is responsible for maintaining the overall standard and compliance of the centre. A Chief Instructor must be in place for each practical discipline. The role of Principal and Chief Instructor may be held by the same person. From an Instructor's point of view the Chief Instructor is responsible for the standards of safety and training and is therefore a crucial contact point and mentor when delivering RYA training.

The Chief Instructor must hold a current RYA Yachtmaster Instructor qualification for sail and/or power as appropriate.

Centre recognition is automatically revoked whenever there is a change of Principal, when active teaching ceases, or if the centre is sold. Centres risk their recognition being withdrawn if, in the opinion of the RYA, the standards set for recognition are not being maintained.

3.1 GAINING RECOGNITION

Before recognition can be granted, the potential Principal must complete the required application form (obtained from RYA Training) and return it with a fee to cover the cost of administration and the initial inspection.

The centre will then be visited by an inspector and, provided the inspector's report is satisfactory, recognition will be granted. The school will then be subject to annual or 'spot' inspections administered by the RYA.

RECOGNITION CONDITIONS

During the inspection, the inspector will expect to see the following:

▶ That the Principal or Chief Instructor holds the relevant and valid RYA Instructor certificate

▶ That the Instructor certificate is supported by a valid and appropriate first aid certificate (see RYA website for details of accepted certificates)

▶ That the centre's teaching course programmes meet the syllabus laid down by the RYA

▶ That the facilities are of a satisfactory standard to support the proposed RYA operation

▶ That the teaching vessels are suitable, appropriate, seaworthy and in good condition

▶ That students are using the correct and appropriate personal buoyancy devices for the courses on offer

▶ That the Principal and/or Chief Instructor fully understands the RYA's requirements necessary for the correct running of an RYA-recognised training centre, especially with regard to advertising and the safe running of certificate and non-certificate courses.

The RYA will then consider the inspector's report and recognise the centre if the report is satisfactory. If an action plan is provided it needs to be completed before recognition is granted.

ADVERTISING AND THE USE OF THE RYA NAME AND LOGO

It is only the Principal that may use the RYA name and logo in any advertising material. Instructors (and examiners) may not do so.

ADMINISTRATION

Once recognition has been granted, Principals may open an account with the RYA to bulk-purchase certificates and RYA publications to be used on courses. The Principal remains responsible for the correct completion, issuing, registering and recording of certificates at the end of courses, and that they are correctly endorsed.

OWN-BOAT TUITION

RYA-recognised training centres may offer own-boat tuition to their customers on the condition that the teaching takes place within the stated operating area of the centre.

The boat used must carry sufficient equipment, particularly safety equipment, to enable the Instructor safely to carry out the training required. Although not everything on the list would necessarily be required, the vessel checklist from the Recognition Guidance Notes should be used as a guide. Additionally, the owner must ensure that their insurance covers them to receive instruction aboard their own boat.

Centres may not offer own-boat courses only.

4 GENERAL CONSIDERATIONS

4.1 DUTY OF CARE

Instructors must always remember that they are sailing with relatively inexperienced people, who may not be able to make a sound assessment of the risks inherent in the activity. Cruising centres must have a clear policy on the use of life jackets. The general position is that life jackets should be worn while on deck, by students and Instructors, while under way unless you are sure they do not need to be. Centres are reminded of the mantra 'Useless unless worn'.

Instructors should not hesitate to require safety lines to be used by crew members when the circumstances make it prudent for them to do so.

4.2 INSTRUCTOR HEALTH DECLARATION

Within the RYA Yachtmaster Scheme, RYA Instructors are required to hold a valid commercial endorsement. It is the Instructor's responsibility to make sure they have an in-date seafarer's medical (ENG1 or ML5) or accepted alternatives as listed on the MCA website. RYA Instructors must declare any medical condition that might affect their duty of care as an Instructor. They also undertake to inform the RYA of any relevant changes in their medical situation after qualifying.

The RYA reserves the right to withhold or suspend qualifications from anyone who is considered unlikely to fulfil this requirement.

4.3 STUDENT HEALTH DECLARATION

So that they are informed as to any additional risk to students, RYA-recognised training centres are strongly advised to include a health declaration in their booking process. The Principal/Chief Instructor must pass on such information to the individual Instructor responsible for the student. The declaration should be designed to ensure that the participants are physically and mentally fit to deal with the particular course for which they have applied.

4.4 RYA LIFE JACKET POLICY

Wear a lifejacket or buoyancy aid unless you are sure you don't need to.

4.5 SWIMMERS

It is strongly recommended that all those participating in the RYA Yachtmaster Scheme should be able to swim. It is essential that the Instructor in charge of a course should know if any members of the course are non-swimmers and should require non-swimmers to wear life jackets at all times when on deck or in a dinghy.

4.6 ALCOHOL CONSUMPTION

While on duty ashore and afloat, practical Instructors are required by law and by the RYA to keep their their alcohol consumption below the maximum permitted for driving road vehicles.

4.7 PRACTICAL AND THEORY COURSES FOR PEOPLE WITH DISABILITIES

All RYA training courses are open to people with disabilities.

There are teaching and enablement issues that sometimes have to be addressed, but all these perceived hurdles disappear when common sense, good practice, reasonable adjustment and seamanship are employed.

There is no better source of information about prospective students than students themselves. The key to good practice is, without doubt, good communication.

The only endorsement now used on certificates is 'Assistance required to complete the course'.

RYA Sailability is always on hand to answer any questions or give advice. Their telephone number is 02380 604247.

5 RYA INSTRUCTOR AWARDS

Who teaches what in the RYA Yachtmaster Scheme?

Instructor Qualification	Qualified to Teach
RYA Keelboat Instructor*	Start Sailing; Basic Skills
RYA Cruising Instructor Sail	Start Sailing; Start Yachting; Competent Crew; Basic Skills; Day Skipper Practical
RYA Cruising Instructor Motor	Start Motor Cruising; Helmsman; Day Skipper Practical
RYA Yachtmaster Instructor Sail	As for RYA Cruising Instructor Sail plus Coastal Skipper and RYA Yachtmaster Coastal/Offshore Preparation
RYA Yachtmaster Instructor Motor	As for RYA Cruising Instructor Power plus Coastal Skipper, Advanced Pilotage, and RYA Yachtmaster Coastal/Offshore Preparation
RYA Cruising Instructor Trainer Sail**	As for RYA Yachtmaster Instructor Sail plus RYA Cruising Instructor (Sail) Training Course
RYA Cruising Instructor Trainer Power**	As for RYA Yachtmaster Instructor Power plus RYA Cruising Instructor (Motor) Training Course
RYA Yachtmaster Instructor Trainer Sail**	As for RYA Cruising Instructor Trainer Sail plus RYA Yachtmaster Instructor (Sail) Training Course and RYA Cruising Instructor/RYA Yachtmaster Instructor Revalidation
RYA Yachtmaster Instructor Trainer Power**	As for RYA Cruising Instructor Trainer Power plus RYA Yachtmaster Instructor (Motor) Training Course and RYA Cruising Instructor/RYA Yachtmaster Instructor Revalidation

* Holding an RYA Yachtmaster Coastal (Sail) Certificate of Competence with a valid commercial endorsement

** RYA Instructor Training courses must only be carried out with the knowledge and permission of the RYA Chief Instructor and must have a moderator

COMMUNICATION BETWEEN THE RYA AND INSTRUCTORS

Wavelength, the RYA's Instructor newsletter, is produced six times a year. Each edition is available electronically on the RYA website at www.rya.org.uk, or as a free download on the RYA ebooks app, which is available on iOS, Android, PCs and Macs.

Information relating to training schemes is distributed in Training Notices and Training Guidance, which are available on the RYA website and included cumulatively in editions of *Wavelength*.

Conferences and short briefings (face-to-face or online via webinars) are held each year for Instructors. These conferences and briefings help Instructors to keep current and allow for feedback and an exchange of ideas. It is strongly recommended that all Instructors should attend a conference or briefing every year. Details are announced via *Wavelength* and on www.rya.org.uk.

In addition to this, all Cruising and RYA Yachtmaster Instructors are required to take a practical revalidation with the RYA before their Instructor certificate expires to ensure they are up to date with the RYA Training Scheme and to verify their continued personal competence.

7 COACHING AND INSTRUCTING TECHNIQUES

Participants in the RYA Yachtmaster Scheme range from young trainees on Tall Ships and skippers learning the intricacies of sailing a 7- to 15-metre yacht to a new owner learning to berth a motorboat. Instructors must have a multitude of skills which have to be adapted to the type of vessel, the type of crew, or the student in the classroom. It is impractical to lay down specific techniques or devise an 'RYA method' in the same way as some of the other RYA training schemes. Here we will look at some of the theory behind instruction. It is intended as guidance for the new Instructor and a reminder for the more experienced of the standards required.

Much of the material has been gained from practical Instructor updates, conferences, Shorebased workshops and talking to the students on the receiving end of the scheme.

7.1 INSTRUCTOR VERSUS COACH?

As an RYA Instructor you will deliver material as both an Instructor and coach. Which of these roles you play depends on a number of factors:

► The type of session (Practical or Theory)

► The subject (new subject or developing existing techniques and skills)

► The teaching method (discussion, demonstration or student practice)

► The environment (ashore or afloat)

► The number of students

► Where the student is within the RYA scheme.

Your role as an Instructor is to help students develop through teaching them practical and theoretical aspects of the relevant syllabus. The lower-level RYA Yachtmaster Scheme Practical courses, up to Day Skipper, predominantly involve explaining and demonstrating techniques that are new to the student – this is the instructing role.

However, the higher-level courses require a shift towards helping students develop techniques into a higher or more automated level. This may require more observation, effective feedback and questioning from the Instructor to help the student develop – this is coaching.

RYA Cruising Instructors can be seen as predominantly instructing; RYA Yachtmaster Instructors are predominantly coaching. However, no training session is ever truly one or the other. We have to learn to use a blend of techniques when we are assessing, instructing, or coaching a session.

7.2 A SIMPLE COACHING MODEL

There are numerous models for structuring training or instruction. A simple view is the Brief-Task-Debrief approach. This gives the general framework of briefing students prior to carrying out an activity (Brief); the students carry out the activity (Task), followed by feedback from the Instructor to identify what they have learnt and going on to explore ways to improve (Debrief). There are many coaching models, each with their own strengths and weaknesses depending on who, what, where or why you are trying to teach. It is common for models to be formed around an acronym: IDEAS or EDICT(S) are two examples which many people may have heard of:

I — **Introduction:** A brief scene setting introduction

D — A clear and accurate **demonstration** or series of demonstrations

E — An **Explanation** to support and enhance the demonstration

A — **Activity** by the student to practice to try out the new topic. Includes feedback from the instructor to improve

S — **Summary** of lessons learnt and of how to improve

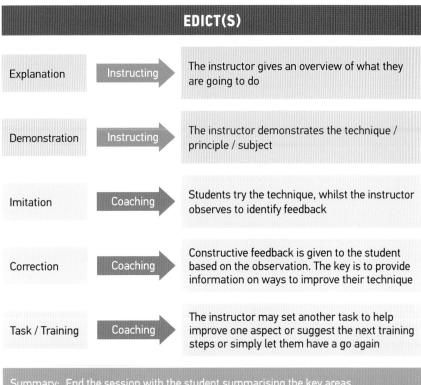

EDICT(S)

Explanation	Instructing	The instructor gives an overview of what they are going to do
Demonstration	Instructing	The instructor demonstrates the technique / principle / subject
Imitation	Coaching	Students try the technique, whilst the instructor observes to identify feedback
Correction	Coaching	Constructive feedback is given to the student based on the observation. The key is to provide information on ways to improve their technique
Task / Training	Coaching	The instructor may set another task to help improve one aspect or suggest the next training steps or simply let them have a go again

Summary: End the session with the student summarising the key areas

The great thing about these models is that it gives a structure to build on when you start your instructing career. Later we will discuss different learning styles and see how these models are helpful in ensuring you match your delivery to a range of learning styles. Your Instructor course will be an opportunity to discuss and try out other models. Look at the EDICT(S) diagram as an example of how the roles of Instructor and coach change throughout any particular session.

7.3 ABOUT STUDENTS AND HOW THEY LEARN

The role of an Instructor is to help the student achieve their goal of learning a new technique or piece of knowledge. Unsurprisingly, it is helpful to know something about how each student learns so we can be effective in our delivery.[1]

RECEIVING AND PROCESSING INFORMATION

Not everyone sees and experiences the world in the same way. We take in information through our senses:

▶ Visually – what we see

▶ Auditory – what we hear

▶ Kinaesthetic – what we touch, feel and experience through movement.

These senses are pathways to our brains. None of us uses one pathway exclusively – there is significant overlap between them – but your students are likely to have a preference.

Visual Learners: Learn through Seeing
They like:

▶ Written information

▶ Pictures, diagrams and observing demonstrations.

They don't like:

▶ Question & answer sessions

▶ Verbal descriptive lessons, e.g. talking though a manoeuvre in detail with no visual reference.

A clue in the language they use that identifies them as visual learners would be "I see what you mean." They can tend to talk quite quickly.

Auditory Learners: Learn through Hearing
They like:

▶ Information contained in the spoken word

▶ Clear verbal explanations/briefings

▶ Verbal feedback

▶ Discussions and question & answer sessions.

They don't like:

▶ Reading to learn.

They can be quite talkative and use language such as "That sounds good."

---

[1]   RYA VAK or VARK model (The 'R' stands for 'Reading')

COACHING AND INSTRUCTING TECHNIQUES

Kinaesthetic Learners: Learn through Doing
They like:
▶ Learning through touch and movement
▶ To 'have a go' and see what happens
▶ Imitation and practice.

They don't like:
▶ Formal lessons with long explanations or hand-outs
▶ Waiting to have a go.

They may stand close when talking with you and are tactile. Although they are keen to have a go, they may not really understand what they are required to do. Be prepared for trial-and-error learning. These are the people who will go first, wanting to get their hands on to learn.

By ensuring our sessions include visual, auditory and kinaesthetic elements to satisfy these three preferences, we should be able to create a learning environment with something for everyone. If you recall the make-up of a coaching model such as EDICT(S) you can see these models are designed to cover each learning style for maximum instructional effect on each session.

Once we have received information we need to process it in order for us to learn. In the same way that we have a preference for absorbing information, we also tend to have a preference for how we learn from this information.

PROCESSING INFORMATION

Just as people have a tendency towards left- or right-handedness, which influences how they tackle manual tasks, many people have a particular learning style which influences how they approach mental tasks.

The way people process the received information can be broken down into 4 groups:

▶ Activists
▶ Reflectors
▶ Theorists
▶ Pragmatists.

Activists

I'll try anything once. They involve themselves fully in new experiences and are very enthusiastic about new learning opportunities. They tend to act first and consider the consequences later, and tackle problems by brainstorming. They are very active, always looking for excitement, and thrive on challenge and new experiences. They can be bored by implementation or consolidation.

They may learn best from self-discovery, learning by doing or trial and error. They will appreciate flexible approaches to learning and generally dislike highly structured approaches or activities that require them to take a passive role.

Reflectors

I'd like time to think about this. They like to ponder experiences and produce observations from different perspectives. They tend to collect data and consider it before reaching conclusions, leading to delay in feedback on issues. They listen to others before making their own point. They may learn best from situations that allow time to research and review what is happening. They like to stand back from events and observe, and learn by listening and sharing ideas with others. They may dislike working to deadlines or having to take immediate action or produce results without much time for planning.

Theorists

How does this fit? They look to make sense of everything, pondering and adapting observations into logical and perhaps complex theories. They tend to think through problems step by step. They like analysis, synthesis and a tidy rational scheme of things. Theorists can feel uncomfortable with subjective judgements, ambiguity and lateral thinking. They may learn best from activities that allow time to integrate observations into theories. They generally like to work independently and normally dislike situations that involve considering feelings or emotions. They dislike those situations, which they consider to be 'shallow'.

Pragmatists

How can I apply this in practice? They tend to think that if it works it's good. They are willing to try out new ideas, theories and techniques to see if they work in practice. They like to get on with things and act quickly and confidently on ideas that attract them. They can be impatient with open-ended discussions.

They may learn best from activities that have clear practical value and that allow ideas and approaches to be tested in practical settings. They will generally like workshop and laboratory teaching methods, and will dislike situations where learning is not directly related to an immediate purpose or obvious relevance.

7.4 COMFORT, STRETCH AND PANIC ZONES

The various elements mentioned so far rely on us adapting to the students' needs. We have no control over what type of learner a student is, only on how we adjust our delivery and teaching style to match their needs. One area that we can change within a student is their emotional state. In simple terms we need to be aware of where our student is mentally. An Instructor may find a passage in heavy weather exhilarating, but a student may find the same trip terrifying, learning nothing or, worse still, being put off for life.

LEARNING ZONES

We can view the student's state in one of three zones: the Comfort Zone, the Stretch Zone and the Panic Zone.

The Comfort Zone is where they, the students, feel comfortable. It tends to be the activity they like doing and are reasonably good at (at least in their own mind!). Although they like being here, it is not the place for them to learn and develop or increase performance. To develop, they need to be pushed into the Stretch Zone. In the Stretch Zone students are slightly outside their Comfort Zone and are being challenged, but with a realistic prospect of

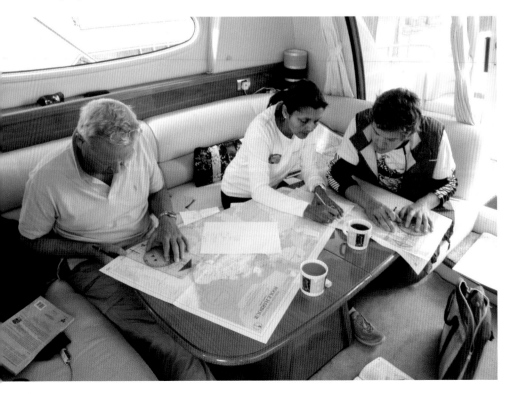

Excited   Willing to risk   Dreaming
Anticipating   Alive   Full of adrenaline
Challenged   Expectant

Safe	STRETCH	Stressed
Lifeless	ZONE	Fearful
Secure		Tense
Stable		Exhausted
Bored	COMFORT	Fed up
Comfortable	ZONE	PANIC	Worried
Unchallenged	ZONE	Anxious
Normal		Disinclined
Easy		Annoyed
Relaxed		Frustrated
Reliable	LEARNING ZONES	Tired

success. Judging how much we are stretching students is an important art for Instructors. Get it right and you build confidence and improve ability. Get it wrong and you risk putting the student into the Panic Zone.

The Panic Zone is all-consuming, and learning is not on the agenda. Once in the Panic Zone it is difficult to get a student out of it. It can destroy confidence and affect skills that were once in the Comfort Zone.

Good training moves the student between the Comfort and Stretch zones, avoiding Panic at all costs. It's easy to see that heavy-weather sailing may be exhilarating for one but frightening for another, but it is often at a much lower level that people edge into the Panic Zone.

Differentiating between each student's needs is important, and ensuring that beginners and advanced students get a fair share of your attention is crucial if we are to deliver and reinforce learning successfully.

CHALLENGE GRAPH

Let's examine how we can do this:

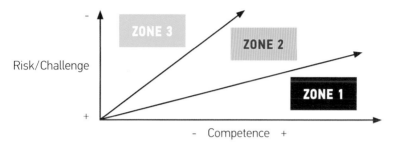

Zone 1 – **Low CHALLENGE/RISK, High COMPETENCE = Boredom**
In this zone, if we do easy tasks, and everything is 'great', there is no development and no growth in the student.

Zone 2 – **CHALLENGE/RISK set to COMPETENCE = Development, peak learning**
In this zone, if we link risk to competence we will create/improve rapport. We will challenge but give the student a sense of adventure, increase development, and create maximum learning.

Zone 3 – **High CHALLENGE/RISK, Low COMPETENCE = Too challenging**
In this zone, if we are too challenging, too hard, set unachievable tasks etc., we will lose rapport and trust. The student will close down and be in the Panic Zone, and therefore there is no learning and no development.

7.5 ACQUIRING A NEW SKILL: THE FOUR STAGES OF COMPETENCE

When looking at a new practical technique, there are four stages that learners typically go through. They may pass through them rapidly or slowly, but everybody will pass through. Having an idea of where a student is in the progression will help identify what they require from you as an Instructor or coach.

STAGE 1 UNCONSCIOUS INCOMPETENCE

The student is unaware (Unconscious) that they are unable to do something (Incompetence): they don't know what they don't know. In this stage the student has no idea that there is a skills gap. This state can exist equally:

1 in a newcomer to the activity who genuinely has a 'beginner's mind' and has not yet experienced any of the techniques or skills required to claim competence, or

2 in an 'experienced' student with a misguided sense that what they are doing is great!

STAGE 2 CONSCIOUS INCOMPETENCE

The student recognises there is a skills gap, and that they want to close it up. They are aware of what they don't know. For some this adds clarity, others find it daunting and frustrating. In general, students need to have entered this stage to be receptive to training.

STAGE 3 CONSCIOUS COMPETENCE

Students are becoming competent but still have to think about what they are doing and how they do it. Following simple sequences will be useful at this stage. Students in this stage will tend to need more coaching than instructing. They know how to do it and can achieve their objective when they concentrate. Refining their technique and moving the skill towards an automated process is how they will progress. Most of the time, practice will make perfect.

STAGE 4 UNCONSCIOUS COMPETENCE

Tasks can be completed with very little conscious thought. Things flow and are effortless. The body moves without any conscious effort, leaving the brain to find new challenges in the quest for improvement. In many ways this is mastery, although people can slip from this level back to Conscious Competence if they do not carry out the technique often enough. This is 'skills fade'.

Tips for Reinforcing Learning

▶ *Always put new techniques into context – understanding is helped if you see the 'big picture'.*

▶ *The average person can deal with approximately seven chunks of information – don't overload them.*

▶ *People remember the beginning and end, but often miss the middle – keep demonstrations and explanations short and structured.*

▶ *Keep information memorable – use unusual, funny or unexpected ways to illustrate your teaching.*

▶ *Use a range of methods to teach important skills in order to cater for your students' range of learning styles, i.e. explaining, showing a video, visualising, reading, looking at pictures, etc.*

▶ *Ensure that new skills become well-established with plenty of practice and reinforcement.*

▶ *Focus your students on what they should do, rather than what they should not do, or they might end up doing the very opposite to what they should!*

7.6 FEEDBACK

As an Instructor you may be tricked into thinking that your main purpose is to instruct, the temptation being constantly to introduce and demonstrate new skills. In actual fact, given all the mediums available to the learner – videos, books, forums – you earn your pay by offering constructive feedback. A student can research a certain skill, watch videos or discuss techniques in online forums, but they can't easily self-diagnose when the skill proves difficult to master on their own. To deliver constructive feedback, you must become a skilled observer.

All Instructors want their students to achieve success. However, once a task has been set, avoid the temptation to correct constantly: allow the student to have a go unhindered. This will give you a good opportunity to observe how much of your teaching has hit the mark.

Top tip: Only step in if it is a question of safety.

OBSERVATION SKILLS

Bearing in mind that the point of your session is either to teach a student a new skill or hone their existing ones, you need to be in a good position to see everything. A skilled observer looks at the whole situation, critically analysing the information.

It is important to use more than just the sense of sight. As experienced skippers, we position a vessel effortlessly; we are in tune with key indicators from our body. Do the revs sound too high for this proximity to the pontoon? Feeling the wind coming from a certain direction, we know whether to speed up or slow down. We must try to convey to our students the sense of noticing slight changes in trim or balance so that they can start to recognise signs other than visual ones, such as the feeling of having slightly borne away or identifying when you've started to accelerate.

During the practice phase, make sure you are in the best position to observe the whole situation (keep an eye outside of the boat) and know what key points you are looking for. Take in the big picture:

► Is it safe?

► Does the student achieve the objective/aim of the session?

► Has the student acknowledged traffic/hazards in the vicinity?

► Are they comfortable and smooth at the helm?

► Is there anything they are doing that, if corrected, would make things more fluid?

► Was everybody briefed and did each person understand what role they were to play?

If the student demonstrates something you were not expecting, remain flexible enough to recognise an equally valid method and give feedback on that. At the end of the task, before delivering your feedback, take a moment to prioritise. Think safety first, then skill acquisition, then 'was it enjoyable?' and finally how they could develop. Any points that relate to safety must be addressed. Consider which key point would have the most significant positive effect when corrected – it may be that it addresses a number of your points in one go.

To start with, you may wish to take notes to jog your memory and help deliver more accurate feedback. These notes may also come in handy at the end of day and end of course review.

DELIVERING FEEDBACK

If we're not careful, feedback can sometimes turn into a monologue. Solutions which are generated by the student are much more likely to be acted upon than those prescribed by the Instructor. Feedback should take the form of a 'coaching conversation', with the student doing most of the talking. Think of it in terms of a radio communication. You need to let go of the transmit button – you have two ears and one mouth, so use them in that ratio!

For various reasons, from how well the student slept the previous night to how windy it is to whether they are feeling hungry, cold or unsafe, the average person can take on between two and seven pieces of information at any one time. With this in mind, try to limit the number of points you wish your students to remember to a maximum of **three**.
On average, we retain just 25–50% of what we hear, so we need to use a variety of methods to engage the student in taking ownership of the feedback process. There are plenty of feedback models to experiment with to find one that suits your style of delivery. However, knowing what message you want the student to take away is the key to success.

At the end of the feedback conversation, the student should be able to summarise what went well and which areas they need to concentrate on for their next session.

MODELS FOR FEEDBACK

The Praise Burger

The top. Give praise for aspects that have gone well. Be specific.

The filling. What's not gone well and how to correct it. Be specific and use the 'rule of 3'. i.e. three key things which at this stage will lead to improvement.

The bottom. More praise, finishing on a positive note.

This is known by varying names, but the point is that a debrief should be rounded in its content. Starting with a "well done" and re-enforcing what went well can break the ice. Follow this with the 'meat' – where and how to improve – before closing on a positive note.

Using Questions: The Traffic Light

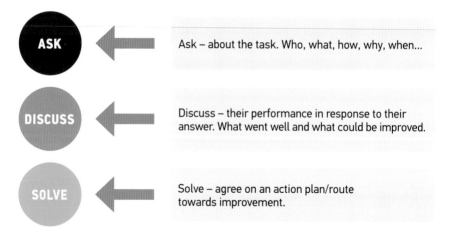

Ask – about the task. Who, what, how, why, when...

Discuss – their performance in response to their answer. What went well and what could be improved.

Solve – agree on an action plan/route towards improvement.

Using questions to elicit feedback from a student works really well, if you ask the right questions! Be wary of half-using questioning by asking something to start the conversation off and then launching into a monologue.

Use questions to get the student to think through their actions. A technique you can use is 'Pose; Pause; Pounce'. Give students time to realise you are posing a question; think about what they know of the subject and then formulate and deliver the answer.

If a student gets the impression that you may crack first and answer the question yourself, they sometime just wait it out. Asking questions in a way that students feel comfortable enough to answer takes time to master. If no response is forthcoming, it is probably because the question is not clear enough.

Using questions in your teaching should be a supportive and friendly way of initiating a coaching conversation. Before you ask, it is good to think, 'will my question get a yes/no response, or do I stand a chance of eliciting more information from the learners?' It might be that you're considering coming alongside for the first time. Think about what would make you feel comfortable enough to contribute. For example: "We'd like to come alongside, we've spoken to the marina office and they've allocated us that berth. Now, before we head on over, what should we think about?" By using this kind of open question, you will encourage participation. Every answer is valid, and you can tease further thoughts from your students.

Be wary of asking closed questions, which can only result in a yes or no answer, as the student is either right or wrong and it leaves little by way of conversation. Students may be put off answering as they may worry about feeling foolish for giving the wrong answer.

CREATING POWERFUL COACHING CONVERSATIONS

There is an art in creating the powerful questions that open up rather than close down coaching conversations. Techniques such as 'the six Ws' or 'Big TED' are two such examples of these.

The Six Ws

These are Rudyard Kipling's six honest serving men: What, Why, When, Who, Where and How. If we start our sentences with these words we cannot help but create an open question. Be careful when using questions starting with "why" as they can appear confrontational.

Big TED:

▶ **T** — Tell Me

▶ **E** — Explain

▶ **D** — Describe

Big TED allows the coach/ Instructor to start the questions and create the really powerful ones, e.g. "Describe how you would come alongside that berth"; "Tell me about that last tack. What did you do with the mainsheet?", etc.

Once we have asked the powerful questions we need to listen carefully to what the students are saying and react to their answers. If we are clever and develop our listening, we can focus on the words they are using and create our questions using the same words in return. For example, if they say "When I did that, I saw..." we could say "Describe what you saw when...", and if they say, "What I heard when this happened was ...", then we could ask "Tell me what happened when you heard...", so we match their language and words. This is a very powerful model if an Instructor develops this.[2]

---

[2] Matching words from the NLP Models (Neuro Linguistic Programming)

Score out of Ten

Another useful technique is to ask the student to score their performance in the task out of ten. At the same time, decide what score you would give. Their answer can sometimes offer a real insight into how confident they are feeling. Their answer can be a good starting point for the conversation.

Even if you don't ask the student to score their manoeuvre out of ten it can be a helpful reference point for you when delivering your feedback. Make sure that the tone of your feedback reflects how well you thought it went. If it was an eight, make sure that most of what you highlight is good! Another tip if using this technique is to use their scoring in your favour. If they mark it a six or seven, ask, "Tell me, what would you do differently it make it a nine or ten?" They then need to think and to provide some solutions for development.

What will you do more of, what will you do less of?

Ask the student to explain what it is that they are going to do less of and what is it that they are going to keep and do more of. This allows them to reflect on the good and bad bits with the Instructor/coach posing the questions, which will highlight the two areas. Again, using 'Big TED' and 'the Six Ws', we can examine and ask them to reflect back on the session aims.

INDIVIDUAL DEBRIEFS THROUGHOUT THE COURSE – MANAGING EXPECTATIONS

Regardless of the techniques you use for debriefing students after each practical session (and there isn't one definitive way), it is important to keep the students informed about their progress throughout the course. Taking the time to speak to the students individually at the end of each day pays dividends at the completion of the course.

Try to keep the daily debriefs fairly short and ensure that you deal with any problems identified during the day as they arise. Think about where to have your chat. The general content should be an appraisal of progress so far, a summary of where to focus the attention during the next day or rest of the course, and an indicator of whether they are on track or not. Be honest, but make sure you leave the possibility of success open. It may take individual students a while to 'get it', but when they do they may well surprise you. Telling a student at the end of day one of a four- or five-day course that they will not pass by the end of the course will not be well received. Telling them that we have a lot of work to do in X, Y or Z to be in with a chance will be more welcome. If, however, halfway through the course it is clear that they are unlikely to complete the whole syllabus successfully, then they need to be advised of this. The end result should not be a surprise.

If you fail to keep them informed then tension will build up on board, with students discussing in whispers whether they are passing or failing. During the final debrief, your teaching may be blamed for the lack of results. This lack of communication between Instructor and student is one of the most common reasons for complaint about RYA courses. Remember that many of the people you teach are highly successful and respected in their own field. The only skill you may have that they haven't is the ability to skipper and instruct. You must ensure they retain their dignity and a positive attitude towards you and the sport. Do not underestimate this part of the job – it is one of the most skilful aspects of instructing.

However, the occasional student can be difficult and disrupt the course. If a student is upsetting the harmony of the course, this cannot be left to resolve itself. You will need to tread carefully. Use questioning to help with this. Discuss one-to-one how the behaviour might be perceived. It is always more powerful if the student can identify what they need to

work on, rather than being told. Try to remain focussed on the disruptive behaviour, and don't get drawn into criticising the person's character. "I noticed when this happened, the atmosphere on board changed, how do you think it made x feel? "

Stick to the facts.

Sometimes nothing works and you have to make the best you can of the week. If you have a difficult student on board, talk to the Principal of the centre as soon as possible. It is often useful to write an account of the course in case the RYA is asked to investigate a complaint.

7.7 COURSE PLANNING

Most centres are situated in areas of sheltered water where courses can continue in virtually any weather. However, in order to give students experience of offshore cruising, you need to spend some time in the open sea. As with recreational cruising, it is a mistake to promise an itinerary at the beginning of the week. The weather and the students' requirements will determine what you do. For example, a group of good dinghy sailors who can handle the boat might benefit from a longer passage through areas of heavy

The table below gives an overview of how Plan-Do-Review (see p.34) affects all elements of delivering RYA training. This will be covered in more detail during your Instructor course.

	Individual Session	For you	For the Student
Plan	What are the key points I want to get across in this session? Does the student have the necessary pre-skills or knowledge for this session? Do you have the necessary stream, wind, depth or boat to do this session?	Have a broad plan of the whole course in terms of the general order of delivery and the locations required to do this. Have a more detailed plan for the next 24–48 hours.	At the start of the course give an overview of what course they are on: "A Day Skipper is…", "We assume you know…", "We will be doing…".
Do	Deliver the session around whatever coaching model you choose. Be flexible enough to change if it isn't working.	Deliver each day in line with your plan, keeping an eye open for learning opportunities such as Collision Regulation examples.	Deliver your training while observing the students' progress.
Review	Did the student retain the key points I wanted to get across? Do I need to change the way I delivered this?	At the end of each day review how well you are progressing along the syllabus and whether you are on track. Be honest about the success and failures. Did I estimate the timings well? Did I miss any key points?	In addition to feedback after particular sessions, the student requires a daily end of day debrief. Highlight what was covered, what went well and where they need to focus. A mid-course debrief should indicate the likelihood of completing the whole course successfully by the end. Be wary of giving this debrief too early just because they had a bad day. At the end of the course, give them guidance on their next steps.

traffic. Good navigators who need boat handling and pilotage practice should stay closer to the land.

Discuss with the Principal good places for teaching, and find out where the yacht is welcome and where it is not. Avoid being too ambitious, particularly on the first day. Even on Coastal Skipper courses the first manoeuvres take longer than you expect. Involve the students as much as possible in the planning.

PULLING IT ALL TOGETHER: PLAN-DO-REVIEW

A key to success is the Plan-Do-Review cycle. This can apply at the higher level of a whole course or at the lower level of an individual session. You start with a plan – your best estimate of how you will deliver the training. You deliver the plan, following it as closely as you can, amending as required. Once done, you review the whole process to see what went well, what didn't and how you might improve the plan.

THE LEARNING ENVIRONMENT

Taking the time to set up an environment conducive to learning will really benefit your students. Put yourself in their position – what could the Instructor do to support my learning? How could they make it easier for me to understand the exercise and all the elements involved?

Ask yourself some questions:

- ▶ Is the boat in a safe position?
- ▶ Can everyone see me without looking into the sun?
- ▶ Can everyone hear me?
- ▶ Is everyone engaged?
- ▶ Do I need to use a different approach using models or a mini whiteboard to explain?
- ▶ What do the students already know that will help them with this exercise?

Linking new skills or knowledge to prior experience is very powerful. It allows learners to establish connections between skills which can help to keep learning relevant. It also gives the learners confidence, as they already know something about the new skill.

An Instructor's instinct is to help their student succeed. This is one of the fundamental reasons behind training to be an Instructor. However, there is a fine line between continual coaching and sailing by voice. It takes a lot of cruising experience to become an Instructor, meaning that you can get a boat to go almost anywhere by directing the helm and crew. If you find yourself wanting to (or actually giving) little bits of information, such as "Five degrees to starboard, slow down...", continually, you may have the impression that the

person on the helm is 'getting it' and is in control, but in reality they are not achieving the task alone. Without the feeling that they are making the decisions, they may just be awaiting your next tip.

If you feel you just can't let the task run without interruption, you may have inadvertently set an exercise that is a bit too complex at this stage in the learning process.

Top tip: Set up for success.

Achieving a successful outcome from a number of less-challenging tasks will form stronger foundations than a lucky first attempt at a more involved task. Allow students to make some mistakes – only step in if safety is in question. Setting appropriate learning opportunities encourages students to use their experience so far and gain confidence.

7.8 YOUR FIRST COURSE

Your best plan is to research the area and arrive early to become familiar with the yacht, and if possible practise handling it before the students arrive. Make a list of the points you wish to make during the safety brief and, at the beginning of each day, make a note of the topics and tasks that you might cover.

When the students arrive, welcome them aboard and ask them about themselves and their experience. Learn their names as soon as possible. Organise the accommodation and explain what you hope to do during the week. Be honest about your experience and invite them to ask you about anything they do not understand. If you come across as sincere and doing your best, the crew will be willing you to succeed even if your technique is unpolished. If you give them an over-inflated view of yourself you will lose their confidence.

If you make an error, admit it, think clearly and put it right. No one gives perfect demonstrations every time, but you should be able to stay in charge and correct a misjudgement. Make sure your navigation and knowledge of the theory is above RYA

Yachtmaster standard. If you are rusty on this, do some revision before the course. Remember your trainee skippers have probably just passed the Shorebased course.

Being slightly nervous before your first course is a good quality. It shows that you care and want to make it a success.

The Principal of the centre is there to give you help and advice. Use it.

On the first day, having covered the safety brief (possibly the evening before), set off as soon as practicable. The first sail hoist or manoeuvre will be slow and inelegant, but the learning curve will be far quicker than on any pre-course theory. Even on an advanced course, deck work and some steering skills will have to be relearnt. Each student will have to be taught individually to some extent; you are acting as a coach rather than a class teacher. Before a new technique, give a clear explanation and demonstration. Help during the manoeuvre, and afterwards debrief the individual or the group, perhaps in the form of asking them whether they thought it went well or whether they would change things next time.

Instructing is tiring, not just physically but more importantly because a yacht skipper has to be continually concerned about the welfare of his crew. Confinement with strangers, while being considerate, fair and pleasant as well as instructing, is exhausting. As you become more experienced the yachting decisions become easier, as does dealing with the people.

At the end of the course, reflecting on of all the things you feel should have done during the week shows you are conscientious – you are evaluating and improving what you do.

7.9 ADVERSE WEATHER

GALES

Sailing Instructors should never be caught out by gales. Sail-training yachts have been screened for stability and can withstand a gale in calm water. In fact, it is often a highlight of the week to sail along a weather shore in a gale. Opportunities for boat handling become less but as soon as the wind moderates a little the storm sails can be used safely for practising manoeuvres without damage.

FOG

Thick fog is the only condition that can bring yachting to a standstill. Radiation (land) fog causes the worst visibility, but fortunately this rarely lasts more than half a day. Advection (sea) fog, which often gives visibility of a few hundred metres, can be regarded as an opportunity for contour navigation. The crew will be as enthusiastic as the Instructor – while you remain positive so will they.

CALM

This is the hardest condition in which to run a sailing course. Your best action is to keep close to the land, practise boat handling and be more ambitious than usual with the pilotage exercises. Avoid long passages under power and avoid scenario games, except perhaps blind pilotage. On spring tides you might be able to use the tide-induced wind, and on the flood tide you should be able to explore creeks and inlets further than usual. Teaching close-quarters handling on a motor cruiser in calm conditions can give learners a false impression of their ability.

ACCIDENTS

Every yachtsman has made errors of judgement. What matters is that you spot the error early and remain in control while you try to solve the problem. In the worst situations, a combination of circumstances may result in the loss of the yacht or a crew member. The subsequent inquiry will ask you searching questions about how you tried to retrieve the situation.

In most cases, cruising centres operate as commercial vessel operators and have a duty to report accidents and incidents to their national authority. For guidance on the incident and accident reporting at your centre, refer to the recognised training centre operating procedures document or safety policy statement.

THE RYA YACHTMASTER SCHEME INSTRUCTOR COURSES

8.1 QUALIFICATION OF PRACTICAL INSTRUCTORS

INSTRUCTOR TRAINING COURSES

During the course the emphasis is on how to teach, rather than how to skipper or crew a yacht. However, each candidate's skippering ability is considered, particularly the skills of pilotage, boat handling and navigation (in the context of setting appropriate tasks and keeping the boat safe during training).

The candidates will be trained in using a range of teaching techniques to deliver RYA courses. The course will be similar in many ways to a normal training course, with skippered passages, sessions on boat handling, and navigation, followed by feedback.

By the end of the course, successful Instructor candidates should be able to generate and maintain interest and communicate clearly on deck and at the chart table.

Some of the problems and complaints received from students on courses arise from inconsiderate and unsympathetic behaviour by the Instructor. Living with different groups of candidates in close quarters requires fortitude and sociability. Aside from introducing boating techniques, the Instructor may need to act as a negotiator or boost a student's morale through a well-timed chat. Instructor candidates who are unable to exhibit appropriate interpersonal skills are unlikely to be successful.

During and at the end of the course, each Instructor candidate is given feedback, which will include the reasons for passing or outlining what needs to be focussed on before having another go. Students should have a good understanding of their own strengths and weaknesses. This is intended to be a positive and constructive method of helping Instructors to develop.

To be successful in any of the Instructor courses candidates must have a high level of subject knowledge. For instance, it would be unlikely that a newly qualified RYA Yachtmaster Offshore would pass an RYA Cruising Instructor course unless already an Instructor in another discipline, and having a very good depth of knowledge. Similarly, an RYA Cruising Instructor applying for an RYA Yachtmaster Instructor course must have gained experience at RYA Cruising Instructor level before attempting to progress. More details of prerequisites can be found on the RYA website (www.rya.org.uk).

9 THE RYA CRUISING INSTRUCTOR COURSE

Courses are delivered in RYA-recognised training centres around the world. The course is taught by one Trainer and moderated on the final day by another one. The Trainers may be RYA Cruising Instructor Trainers or RYA Yachtmaster Instructor Trainers.

Prerequisites:

▶ Hold a commercially endorsed RYA Yachtmaster Offshore Certificate of Competence (with all associated certification in date)

▶ Hold a valid first aid certificate which is accepted by the RYA (go to www.rya.org.uk)

▶ Successfully complete RYA Professional Practices and Responsibilities (PPR) Course, even if not required for commercial endorsement until next revalidation of commercial endorsement

▶ Candidates must enrol on and pass the online pre-course RYA Cruising Instructor Theory test (incorporating teaching background theory and RYA Yachtmaster Offshore Theory).

Pre-entry syllabus

Theory knowledge assessment to RYA Yachtmaster Offshore.

Teaching and learning theory

▶ How students learn
  • Learning styles
  • Stages of learning

▶ Barriers to learning
  • Comfort/Stretch/Panic

▶ Neurolinguistic Programming

▶ Simple coaching models and their uses and limitations

▶ Questioning techniques.

Structuring feedback

▶ Observation skills

▶ Prioritising feedback – safety-learning-fun.

PRACTICAL COURSE SYLLABUS

Plan-Do-Review

▶ Plan
  • Structuring a lesson
  • Identifying achievable tasks/transferable method
  • Identifying key teaching points
  • Prerequisite knowledge
  • Logical order of delivery
  • Location and time management – planning v. opportunism
  • Use of teaching aids

▶ Do
  • EDICT(S) as a benchmark to discuss, but not restricted to using this model

▶ Review
  • Self-review.

RYA Orientation

▶ Operating procedures

▶ Centre policies

▶ Role of RYA Cruising Instructor/Chief Instructor/Principal

▶ Dealing with complaints.

THE RYA CRUISING INSTRUCTOR COURSE

Debriefing/Feedback Skills

▶ Observation skills

▶ Feedback

▶ Prioritising – safety/learning/fun

▶ Action Plans.

Catastrophe Clinic

▶ Avoiding pitfalls

▶ Learning from accidents/incidents.

ASSESSMENT CRITERIA

Practical Courses

Knowledge of:

Start Sailing, Start Yachting, Competent Crew, Basic Skills, Start Motor Cruising, Helmsman, and Day Skipper Shorebased and Practical courses.

Understands:

▶ RYA programme of courses

▶ Levels of competence required for award of the above certificates.

Instructional Technique

Can:

▶ Set up tasks and teaching sessions appropriate to individual students

▶ Brief clearly

▶ Ensure tasks are undertaken correctly and safely

▶ Observe the task and note areas requiring improvement

▶ Debrief students and agree an achievable plan for improvement

▶ Demonstrate any part of the Start Sailing, Start Yachting, Competent Crew, Basic Skills, Start Motor Cruising, Helmsman, and Day Skipper Practical courses

▶ Explain the practical application of any part of the Day Skipper Shorebased Course.

Interpersonal Skills

▶ How to give and receive feedback.

SAIL

Qualifying courses for RYA Cruising Instructors can be run at any centre with sail cruising recognition, but must be taught and moderated by RYA Cruising Instructor Trainers or RYA Yachtmaster Instructor Trainers. The course is five days in duration.

POWER

Qualifying courses for RYA Cruising Instructors can be run at any centre with motor cruising recognition, but must be taught and moderated by RYA Cruising Instructor or RYA Yachtmaster Instructor Trainers. The course is four days in duration.

REVALIDATION

Both sail and power Instructors must attend a revalidation course at least every five years to retain their qualification. If issued, the Instructor endorsement can be valid for five years, at the RYA's discretion. Revalidations of both RYA Cruising Instructor and RYA Yachtmaster Instructor qualifications are given by RYA Yachtmaster Instructor Trainers.

Due to the arduous nature of practical training afloat, an Instructor Endorsement obtained or revalidated after the Instructor's 67th birthday will require revalidation with effect from the Instructor's 72nd birthday. An Instructor Endorsement obtained or revalidated after the Instructor's 70th birthday will be valid for a period of two years before a further update is required.

10 THE RYA YACHTMASTER INSTRUCTOR COURSE

Courses are delivered by the RYA. The course is taught by one Trainer and moderated on the final day by another one. The Trainers will be RYA Yachtmaster Instructor Trainers.

Prerequisites:

▶ Hold a commercially endorsed RYA Yachtmaster Offshore

▶ Hold an RYA Cruising Instructor qualification

▶ One year's practical teaching experience recommended

▶ Successfully complete RYA Professional Practices and Responsibilities (PPR) Course, even if not required for commercial endorsement until next revalidation of commercial endorsement

▶ Have more than 7,000 miles logged.

PRACTICAL COURSE SYLLABUS

▶ Revision of RYA Cruising Instructor Course and understand change in emphasis from instructing beginners to coaching more experienced students

▶ Know the responsibilities of a Principal/Chief Instructor

▶ Understand the ethos of the RYA

▶ Peer learning

▶ Be able to review teaching/ instructing ability

▶ Understand the coaching cycle:
  • Involvement of the whole group
  • Observe – identify the root cause of problems
  • Tweak and improve techniques, not rebuild in your own image

▶ Be able to identify prior learning of students

▶ Obtain early assessment of current ability (start point)

▶ Have knowledge of multiple coaching/teaching techniques

▶ Understand higher-level practical and theoretical techniques – teaching practice

▶ Include Shorebased delivery input:
  • How to teach (theory/ classroom techniques)
  • Lesson planning
  • Structure
  • Presentation skills.

11 ORGANISING PRACTICAL COURSES

11.1 SAILING COURSES

Course	Length
Start Sailing	Two days
Start Yachting	Two days
Competent Crew[1][2]	Five days
Basic Skills	Two days
Day Skipper Practical[2][3]	Five days
Coastal Skipper[2]	Five consecutive days
RYA Yachtmaster Coastal/Offshore Preparation[4][5]	Suggested as a five-day course

Notes:

1   Five consecutive days, three weekends or a two- and three-day weekend.
2   Must be residential.
3   Five consecutive days or three weekends.
4   RYA Yachtmaster Coastal and RYA Yachtmaster Offshore Preparation courses must be run by an RYA Yachtmaster Instructor. Although not an official RYA course and with no specific syllabus due to the bespoke nature, it must be run within the ethos and spirit of the recognition guidelines.
5   Although the student/instructor ratio is 5:1, please remember that only four RYA Yachtmaster candidates can be examined in any one session.

COURSE COMBINATIONS

Course	Can combine with
Start Sailing	Bespoke course
Start Yachting	Competent Crew, Day Skipper
Competent Crew	All RYA certified courses
Basic Skills	Bespoke course
Day Skipper Practical	Competent Crew
Coastal Skipper	Competent Crew
RYA Yachtmaster Coastal/Offshore Preparation	Suggested as a stand-alone course[1]
RYA Yachtmaster Coastal/Offshore exam	Stand-alone exam – do not combine with RYA courses

Note:

1   RYA Yachtmaster candidates may require intensive coaching, which can make combining RYA Yachtmaster Preparation with other courses difficult. Unless each student's needs are closely considered, there is a high chance that no one will have a successful course.

GENERAL CONSIDERATIONS FOR COURSE PLANNING

The student/Instructor ratio must not exceed 5:1. Any customers on board for other reasons (e.g. to gain experience or mileage) are included in this ratio.

All courses, with the exception of Start Yachting, should last a minimum of 103 hours. Typically, if this was a Monday to Friday course, this would be 0900hrs on the Monday until 1600hrs on the Friday. During the course the yacht should sail a minimum of 100 miles, including four night hours (with the exception of Start Sailing, Start Yachting and Basic Skills).

The Instructor should plan an itinerary, taking into account the ability of the crew, the weather conditions, and the requirements to cover the syllabus in an interesting, varied and informative way. It is unacceptable for a boat to day sail from her home port throughout the course.

The Instructor should sleep on board for a minimum of four nights.

Each student should experience at least four hours of night watch-keeping.

With the possible exceptions of Competent Crew and Watch Leader, all RYA Yachtmaster Scheme courses should be delivered on vessels under 15m.

11.2 MOTOR COURSES

The student to Instructor ratio must not exceed 5:1.

Course	Length
Start Motor Cruising[1]	Two days
Helmsman[1]	Two days
Day Skipper Practical[1]	Four days
Advanced Pilotage[1,2]	Two days
Coastal Skipper[3]	Five days
RYA Yachtmaster Coastal/Offshore Preparation[4,5]	Suggested as a four- or five-day course

Notes:

1 May be non-residential, but evening sessions will be required to cover the syllabus.

2 Student to Instructor ratio 3:1.

3 Must be residential and each student should experience four hours of night watch-keeping.

4 RYA Yachtmaster Coastal and RYA Yachtmaster Offshore Preparation courses must be run by an RYA Yachtmaster Instructor. Although not an official RYA course and with no specific syllabus due to the bespoke nature, it must be run within the ethos and spirit of the recognition guidelines.

5 Although the student/instructor ratio is 5:1, please remember that only four RYA Yachtmaster candidates can be examined in any one session.

COMBINED COURSES

Course	Can combine with
Start Motor Cruising	All RYA certified courses
Helmsman	Start Motor Cruising or Day Skipper
Day Skipper Practical	Start Motor Cruising or Helmsman
Advanced Pilotage	Start Motor Cruising. Student to Instructor ratio 3:1 (max.) on Advanced; 2:1 on Start Motor Cruising
Coastal Skipper	Start Motor Cruising
RYA Yachtmaster Coastal/Offshore Preparation	Suggested as a stand-alone course[1]
RYA Yachtmaster Coastal/Offshore exam	Stand-alone exam – do not combine with RYA courses

Note:

1   RYA Yachtmaster candidates may require intensive coaching, which can make combining RYA Yachtmaster Preparation with other courses difficult. Unless each student's needs are closely considered, there is a high chance that no one will have a successful course.

GENERAL CONSIDERATIONS FOR COURSE PLANNING

The student to Instructor ratio must not exceed 5:1 (for Advanced Pilotage 3:1). Any customers on board for other reasons (e.g.to gain experience or mileage) are included in this ratio.

During the course the motor cruiser should travel a minimum of 100 miles, including four night hours (with the exception of Start Motor Cruising, Helmsman and Advanced Pilotage).

The Instructor should plan an itinerary, taking into account the ability of the crew, the weather conditions and the requirements to cover the syllabus in an interesting, varied and informative way.

If the Helmsman's Course and Day Skipper Course are combined, the duration of the combined course may be five days.

11.3 PRACTICAL COURSE BRIEFING

SAFETY BRIEFING

▶ Before the commencement of any voyage the skipper should ensure that all persons on board are briefed, as a minimum, on the stowage and use of personal safety equipment such as lifejackets, thermal protective aids and lifebuoys, and the procedures to be followed in cases of emergency.

▶ In addition to these requirements, the skipper should ensure at least one other person onboard is familiar with the following:

a Location of liferafts and the method of launching;

b Procedures for the recovery of a person from the sea;

c Location and use of pyrotechnics;

d Procedures and operation of radios carried on board;

e Location of navigation and other light switches;

f Location and use of firefighting equipment;

g Methods of starting, stopping, and controlling the main engine;

h Methods of navigating to a suitable port of refuge.

i Location of Stability Guidance Booklet, and Stability Information Booklet if applicable.

In addition to the above, the initial course briefings should include:

Course

Aims	The importance of clothing and boots
Programme	Seasickness
Details of students' experience – are they swimmers?	

Safety

Harnesses and jackstay	Crew action for MOB, fire, and flood
Gas routine (put the kettle on)	

Husbandry

Gear stowage and tidiness	Heads and seacocks

Cruising Vessel

Basic layout below

Fresh water

Electrics

Engine operation

Before Departure

Stow gear ready for sea

Basic engine checks

12 THE RYA YACHTMASTER SCHEME COURSES

To be used in conjunction with the RYA Yachtmaster Scheme Syllabus & Logbook.

12.1 ASSESSING YOUR STUDENTS' ABILITIES

There is an element of assessment in every RYA training course; not just the formal assessment that leads to the award of a certificate but the more informal assessment that takes place throughout the course, no matter how short or long it may be. Assessment is about understanding how the student is performing against a set of standards or expectations.

This might be summarised in three stages:

▶ Initial assessment

▶ Formative assessment

▶ Summative assessment

For example, when an Instructor first meets their students an 'initial assessment' takes place, where the Instructor tries to establish what experience and skills the students already have. The initial assessment may be a simple discussion of previous cruising experience, or it may be made slightly more formal by asking students to set out on paper what they have done previously. The first practical session is also used to establish the starting point for the course. The benefit of this approach is to enable you to structure the course and the content to suit the students' actual levels of ability rather than their assumed level. There may also be formal checks to be made on pre-course requirements for Instructor training.

As the course progresses, you will be carefully monitoring students' progress to see if the pace is too fast, too slow or just right to be challenging, informative and achievable. This can be described as 'formative assessment' and once again could be either formal or informal. Group discussions, quizzes and one-to-one discussions may be useful here.

Finally, at the end of the course, you have to decide, with the help of the Chief Instructor, whether or not the objectives of the training have been achieved. This is the 'summative assessment' and once again could use a range of methods to achieve an objective view of the assessment criteria. However, it will be based almost entirely on whether the student 'can' perform a skill successfully or not without input. Ultimately, the question will be whether to award the certificate. To help you in this the following statements or measures may be of use, but never forget that most people are taking training for fun, and recognising the progress your students have made by the award of certificates is more likely to motivate them to continue than withholding the certificate because they cannot perform the task every time!

Courses are continually assessed; Instructors should take note of the levels of delivery required as detailed in the logbook. The syllabuses now have three specified levels of teaching to show you the depth to which you need to cover each item.

These levels are:

KNOWLEDGE OF THE SUBJECT

The subject will be briefly explained. Familiarisation will occur during the course and information on where to find out more will be given.

UNDERSTANDS THE SUBJECT

The subject will be covered in greater depth. The student will be asked to demonstrate a basic understanding and go away from the course able to develop further their own skill in this area. Confirmation of their understanding of the subject may be achieved in a number of ways during the course.

CAN DEMONSTRATE A LEVEL OF PROFICIENCY IN THE SUBJECT

The subject will be covered in great depth, including background theory, practical demonstrations by the Instructor and repeated practice by the student until they can demonstrate good skills in the subject.

12.2 CERTIFICATES

RYA certificates provide a great incentive to continue training, providing a clear measure of an individual's progress. However, they can become a discouragement to the weak student as the prospect of gaining a certificate fades. It is of utmost importance to keep everyone informed of their progress through the course. The door of possibility should be left open, but an honest and realistic appraisal of where the students are and what they will have to work on should be given regularly throughout the course. As an Instructor, you should explain what can be achieved and agree with the student on how to get the most out of the course.

Throughout the course you should set goals, point out strengths and weaknesses and offer encouragement. They should help the student to recognise how much has been achieved as the course progresses so that by the final debrief they are not surprised by the outcome, whether pass or defer, and they feel satisfied that the course was worthwhile.

12.3 THE COURSES

The RYA Yachtmaster Scheme is split into two types of course: skills, and cruising courses.

12.4 SKILLS COURSES

These courses are best taught as stand-alone courses where everyone on board is taking the same training. These courses focus on learning specific techniques and students can expect plenty of time getting hands-on practice at each given skill.

Skills courses are not necessarily aimed only at newcomers to the Yachtmaster scheme. They can be taken at any time to enhance knowledge and experience in a particular area of interest.

SAILING SKILLS: START SAILING – LEVEL 1

By the end of this course the student will have a basic understanding of yacht handling under sail, including practical techniques and background knowledge. Although this course is delivered on a yacht its focus is a course delivered under sail and getting to grips with the concept of sailing rather than on living on a yacht and sail cruising.

SAILING SKILLS: BASIC SKILLS – LEVEL 2

On completion of this course, students will have a basic knowledge of sailing and be capable of sailing a yacht in light winds as crew and helm with a skipper on board. Although this course is delivered on a yacht its focus is a course delivered under sail rather than focusing on living on a yacht.

It is assumed that every student starting this course has already mastered the practical skills and absorbed the background knowledge required for Start Sailing – Level 1. Both courses can be combined, which will then count towards two days of a Competent Crew course.

START YACHTING (SAIL)

This course provides a short introduction for novices to sail cruising. By the end of the course participants will have experienced steering a yacht, sail handling, ropework, and be aware of safety on board.

START MOTOR CRUISING (MOTOR)

This course aims to introduce the skills required to be useful crew and allow students to gain an understanding of how they can assist the skipper.

HELMSMAN (MOTOR)

By the end of this course the student should be able to manoeuvre a motor vessel confidently. This course provides familiarisation for someone looking to get to know their new boat with the benefit of having an experienced Instructor on board.

ADVANCED PILOTAGE (MOTOR)

By the end of this course, the student should have the skills and techniques required to be able to pilot a motor cruising vessel safely using a variety of means, including radar by day and night. A student undertaking this course might not yet have the experience required for Coastal Skipper.

WHAT'S THE OUTCOME? ADVANCED PILOTAGE

The student is a former owner of a 26' sportsboat who has recently upgraded to a 42' sports cruiser. He has completed Powerboat Level 2, Day Skipper Shorebased, and RYA Yachtmaster/Coastal Skipper Shorebased, along with numerous short courses. His RYA Yachtmaster/Coastal Skipper Shorebased course was some 20 years previous. His boat handling and skippering by day was good, however he struggled considerably at night. He quickly became disoriented, and ran aground twice.

DECISION

All sections signed apart from night cruising. It is clear that the student requires another session with an Instructor to boost his skill set at night before the Advanced Pilotage certificate can be awarded.

12.5 CRUISING COURSES

The emphasis on these courses is living on board a cruising vessel. Skippering skills such as managing the crew and running the boat, practical pilotage and passage planning are integral parts of the courses and, as such, rather than focussing on hard-skills acquisition (like the Skills courses) the courses are more holistic.

The trickier aspect of cruising courses for an Instructor is assessing whether an individual has satisfied all aspects of the syllabus. Although these courses are continually assessed against the syllabus as detailed in the logbook, Day Skipper and Coastal Skipper are command courses where there is a requirement to prove competence in vessel-management skills. The decision as to whether or not a candidate is successful is made bearing all of the above in mind. Individual debriefs, occurring regularly throughout the course, will shape your perception of how a student is progressing. Making notes throughout the course will help you keep track of an individual's progress. The result of the course should reflect an overall impression gathered of the student's ability and progress over the entire course.

COMPETENT CREW (SAIL)

By the end of this course the student should be a useful member of the crew of a cruising yacht. This course introduces a complete beginner to cruising and teaches personal safety, seamanship and basic helmsmanship.

Students who hold a keelboat certificate under the National Sailing Scheme can gain a Competent Crew certificate by completing a further three days or two weekends on a cruising yacht.

WATCH LEADER

The Watch Leader course is conducted on board a large cruising vessel (over 15m Length Overall (LOA)) or a motor/sail training vessel to teach watch-keeping, seamanship and navigation up to the standards required for taking charge of a watch on deck, at sea or in harbour, under the supervision of a deck officer.

DAY SKIPPER COURSE (SAIL OR MOTOR)

By the end of this course the student should have the necessary skills in pilotage, navigation, seamanship and boat handling to skipper a small cruising vessel safely, by day, in waters with which the student is familiar.

WHAT'S THE OUTCOME? DAY SKIPPER SAIL

Student A

Student A works for a large company in a non-sailing location. His firm regularly organises training activities at its premises and afloat. His Day Skipper Practical training was due to be completed over a three-day weekend, followed by a two-day weekend. On the first Friday evening he didn't arrive at the yacht until 2300hrs, blaming work. For the second weekend he failed to arrive until 0900hrs on the Saturday morning. Throughout all the days he was preoccupied with his smartphone, and seemed to be spending much of his time talking to friends as well as working. In the evenings he was always the first off the yacht, and insisted on meals ashore with extended time in the pub. He was very reluctant to complete any night exercise. He refused to get involved in the yacht husbandry and daily routines. When he was participating, he had a tendency to get frustrated and refuse to refine tasks with a second attempt.

Decision

This candidate has not completed the required number of hours afloat. He needs a debrief on how to be more involved in on-board life, and he needs some further days of training before a certificate can be awarded.

Student B

Student B is a 'fast-track' candidate who is on a 16-week RYA Yachtmaster programme. He has done a lot of dinghy sailing and was very confident on deck. He struggled massively with anything theoretical, from filling in the log to weather and IRPCS. He is due to attend a seven-day mile-builder followed by his RYA Yachtmaster/Coastal Skipper Shorebased (which he is extremely concerned about, as 'classrooms don't work for him').

Decision

Sign all sections of the logbook with the exception of Navigation; Pilotage; Meteorology; Rules of the Road, and Passage Making. Give the student a positive debrief that focuses on his sailing skills and stresses the need to find a way of closing the gaps in his knowledge. Provide him with some written notes to take to his subsequent Instructors.

Student C

Student C is a successful small-business owner, who has decided in later life to take up sailing and booked onto a number of courses, culminating in the nine-day combined Day Skipper Shorebased & Practical Course. She is used to managing a team of 20 people in a busy, open-plan, active environment, and is extremely confident and loud. She passed the first four days of classroom training with relative ease, but was not aware of her weaker areas. She immediately took charge on arrival on the yacht, and continually attempted to set the pace, programme, and allocate tasks to the rest of the crew. She carried out several safe micro-navigation exercises, including a tricky pilotage into a poorly marked harbour. During debriefs she paid little attention to feedback, and it was clear she felt she had nothing to learn.

Decision

Pass, with a thorough debrief on the need to develop continually and refine techniques. While her personality may have made the week challenging for the Instructor, she was technically safe and completed all aspects of the course.

Student D

An overweight gentleman, Student D owns and lives aboard a large wheelhouse yacht. He has plans to cruise around the world, and has 'finally got around to doing the Day Skipper'. He attended Shorebased night school and was a conscientious learner, if not the fastest. On arrival at the yacht he struggled to get on board, and explained that he had steps and a gate by his own boat. Very early on in the week it was identified that he lacked both the physical strength and the endurance to play a fully active role in the running of the yacht. He very rarely left the cockpit, and when carrying out manoeuvres such as anchoring, mooring buoys, and berthing/unberthing, he could not be relied upon to carry out tasks with any sort of speed. His sail trim was instinctive and effective, and his power handling always took into account wind and tide, and was a joy to watch. Below decks he was an effective crew member, and was quite handy with maintenance tasks.

Decision

Pass, with a very careful debrief. He has successfully completed all areas of the course, but needs to be aware of his own limitations as regards strength, endurance, and mobility. With his strengths identified, moving forwards he needs to focus on how he remains safe on board, and gets the most out of his boating.

Students E & F

Students E & F have bought a 46' flybridge motor cruiser. They are a husband and wife team. He (student E) tends to overcomplicate things, and gets very shouty in close proximity to other craft. He passed his Day Skipper Shorebased course with flying colours, but he struggles to translate that to practical applications. He had not completed any prior training, although he did complete a two-day handover with the boat broker.

Student F, his wife, is very nervous, and expressed several times how little she wanted to be on the course. She had not attended a Shorebased course, and stated that navigation was too complicated, and it's her husband's role. She has refused to allow their children on board until her husband has achieved his Day Skipper Practical.

Decision

Student E: Pass with careful debrief. Point out to him that motor cruising should be enjoyable, and he has bought the boat to help his family enjoy their leisure time. Encourage him to complete some guided/support trips to help bridge the gap between theory and practical. Technically he was safe, and he completed all sections of the course adequately.

Student F: Expectations need to be managed here, preferably before the final day of the course. Student F has not met the prerequisites on Shorebased knowledge, and simply awarding the certificate would achieve nothing. Depending on which areas of the course she took an active role in, it may be more appropriate to award the Start Motor Cruising and/or Helmsman's certificates.

Student G

Student G attended an RYA Day Skipper course on a sea school motor cruiser during a week of strong winds and occasional heavy rain. All the candidates on the course struggled with the boat-handling elements, particularly student G. In the odd moments where there was a lull he had great successes on a variety of berths, but his confidence quickly diminished when the wind blew again. His theoretical knowledge and seamanship/skippering skills were good, as was his practical navigation and pilotage.

Decision

Pass, with positive debrief. He has demonstrated an understanding of the elements, and is aware of his boat-handling limitations. Technically he was safe and he completed all sections of the course adequately.

COASTAL SKIPPER (SAIL OR MOTOR)

By the end of this course the student should have the skills and techniques required to be able to skipper a cruising vessel safely on coastal and offshore passages by day and night.

WHAT'S THE OUTCOME? COASTAL SKIPPER SAIL

Student H

Completed her Competent Crew and Watch Leader training aboard a large sail-training vessel. She has thousands of sea miles but none on a vessel under 20m. Throughout the week she struggled with boat handling and manoeuvring, and tended to overcomplicate sail evolutions. She was very bossy with the other candidates, and alienated herself very quickly. Her navigation and pilotage was strong, but she struggled to carry out man-overboard manoeuvres under either sail or power. She has a tendency to cover any weaknesses by saying "well, on xyz yacht, we do it like this", and has proven very closed off to different ideas.

Decision

Sign all sections except for Passage Making and Ability as Skipper; Yacht Handling under Power, and Emergency Situations. Give a careful debrief that makes it clear her previous experience is valuable, but stress the need to gain skills on smaller craft before completing the Coastal Skipper training.

Student I

Student I has 'sailed all his life', and is a boat owner (34' deep keel traditional yacht). He has not completed any formal Shorebased training, and has stepped in at Coastal Skipper as he feels Day Skipper is beneath him. Planning and navigation skills were very weak, and secondary port calculations and pilotage were an absolute revelation to him, although he did have some stronger navigational knowledge. Good natured and cheerful, he was enthusiastic about how much he was learning over the week, and how he should have done the course years ago. He told frequent stories of boating mishaps that had occurred on his yacht, and seemed delighted to learn.

Decision

Recommend a 'back to basics' approach. With Student I's honest integrity, it's clear he has identified the gaps in his own knowledge which weren't apparent to him before. Publications such as the RYA Navigation Exercises book would help prepare him for an RYA Yachtmaster/Coastal Skipper Shorebased course, and the Day Skipper Practical course would help fill in the gaps on pilotage, skippering, and seamanship. Fill in the voyage details of his logbook, but do not sign off sections of the Coastal Skipper syllabus.

WHAT'S THE OUTCOME? COASTAL SKIPPER MOTOR

Student J

Student J is a superyacht deckhand. She has not attended any Day Skipper training, and she completed the RYA Yachtmaster Shorebased course online less than 10 days before the start of her Coastal Skipper training. She attended the Coastal Skipper Practical course as a precursor to the RYA Yachtmaster Offshore exam. Theoretical knowledge was good; however, command skills, small craft seamanship, and boat handling were weak. She tended to get flustered when under pressure, and displayed a reluctance to make decisions. When decisions were made, they were often poor/unsafe. She has spent the week blaming the boat and Instructor for their shortcomings, and keeps repeating that if she doesn't pass the RYA Yachtmaster Coastal exam the following week, she will lose her job.

Decision

All sections signed apart from section 4, Passage Making and Ability as Skipper, and Section 6, Boat Handling. The debrief should focus on the unsafe decisions. It should also include a look ahead to the RYA Yachtmaster Offshore preparation and exam, and student J should be encouraged to gain as much small-craft experience as possible before attempting this. It is likely that if the student met the offshore skippering prerequisites this would solve the problem.

Student K

Student K is relatively new to motor cruising. He completed an RYA Start Motor Cruising course two months ago, followed immediately by the Helmsman's course, Powerboat Level 2, Day Skipper Shorebased, Day Skipper Practical, RYA Yachtmaster/Coastal Skipper Shorebased, Radar, Diesel, SRC, First Aid, and Sea Survival courses. He was technically competent, but his lack of experience showed, especially when the unexpected happened.

Decision

Pass, with careful debrief. He needs to be clear on the need to gain further experience outside of the training world. He was technically competent, showed a willingness to learn, and was safe.

13 QUALIFICATION OF INSTRUCTORS FOR TEACHING SHOREBASED COURSES

An effective Instructor must have credibility with students and a genuine interest and engagement with the subject is essential for this. Questions from students will often stray outside the core syllabus or be concerned with seeking advice about equipment or situations. Without enthusiasm and a depth of knowledge far above the RYA syllabus, this credibility could easily be lost. It is difficult to quantify in writing exactly what this means but without extensive practical experience of the subject, candidates are unlikely to be successful on this Instructor course. Due to time constraints on Shorebased Instructor courses there is limited opportunity to fill any gaps in knowledge. As such, Shorebased Instructor courses are a blend of assessing the candidate's knowledge and instructing ability, and ensuring the structure and standard required of the course is understood. Candidates must therefore ensure they have sufficient underpinning knowledge prior to attending a Shorebased Instructor course.

Candidates for Shorebased Instructor courses should be an RYA Instructor in a practical discipline.

13.1 CONDUCT OF SHOREBASED COURSES

RYA Shorebased courses shall be run only by establishments recognised by the RYA.

RYA recognition depends on:

1. There being a suitably qualified Instructor.
2. There being a suitably equipped teaching room which will allow all the students to do chartwork simultaneously and has computer and audio/visual facilities.

The Principal of the centre is responsible for ensuring that adequate standards of tuition are maintained, and that minimum teaching time is met.

13.2 NAVIGATION INSTRUCTOR

The Navigation Instructor course is two days in duration and covers teaching navigation theory in a classroom. There is plenty of practice at delivering and watching short sessions. Candidates should come away from the course with a good number of ideas of different methods for delivering sessions to engage their learners.

Candidates' knowledge should be in excess of the RYA Yachtmaster Shorebased certificate and they are advised to work through the Shorebased papers that are sent out prior to the course.

Successful completion allows the candidate to teach Shorebased navigation up to and including Coastal Skipper/RYA Yachtmaster Offshore Theory.

Candidates should hold the RYA/MCA Yachtmaster Offshore Certificate of Competence or be an Advanced Powerboat Instructor, and have successfully completed the Coastal Skipper/RYA Yachtmaster Offshore Shorebased Certificate in the last five years.

Shorebased Instructor course dates are published on the RYA website, where further information on all RYA Shorebased courses can be found.

13.3 SRC ASSESSOR

The two-day course focuses on training candidates both to teach the SRC course and to assess candidates on a course run by another SRC Instructor.

In order to attend the SRC Assessor course, candidates must hold the SRC short range certificate themselves and already be an RYA Instructor in another discipline such as cruising, powerboat or dinghy. Some other specialist groups may also be considered.

Short range certificate assessor courses are organised on a regional basis. A list of courses and regional organisers can be downloaded from the RYA website.

13.4 RADAR INSTRUCTOR

The one-day Radar Instructor course covers all aspects of delivering the RYA Radar course. Potential Instructors must be experienced in the use of small marine radar for collision avoidance and pilotage, and their knowledge should be well in excess of the RYA's Radar course. Candidates should hold one of the following: RYA Advanced Powerboat Instructor; RYA Cruising Instructor; RYA Yachtmaster Instructor.

Courses are organised centrally by the RYA. See the website for details.

13.5 DIESEL ENGINE MAINTENANCE INSTRUCTOR

The one-day Diesel Instructor course is a hands-on course looking at techniques for teaching the ins and outs of a diesel engine.

Potential Instructors should have a good knowledge of the operation and maintenance of marine diesel engines. Candidates who come from an automotive background should be familiar with both direct and indirect marine cooling systems and salt-water filtration.

13.6 FIRST AID INSTRUCTOR

The one-day First Aid Instructor course allows candidates to deliver parts of the syllabus and gain ideas on how to deliver other areas through observing the other candidates' sessions and via input from the Trainer.

Applicants for Instructor training must hold the First Aid at Work certificate, or an equivalent, as a minimum First Aid qualification. Once qualified, an in-date advanced First Aid certificate (minimum First Aid at Work) must be held. Doctors and nurses with recent appropriate acute experience, and paramedics are exempt from the need for a First Aid certificate, but attending an RYA First Aid course before attending the Instructor course is highly recommended. Once retired and no longer practising, a full First Aid certificate will be required after three years. In addition, all applicants must hold a VHF or SRC certificate and are normally expected to be an RYA Instructor in another field. Special cases may be considered.

The RYA Sea Survival course and certified training in the use of an Automatic External Defibrillator (AED) is highly recommended for all potential First Aid Instructors.

Instructors must be able to appreciate the restrictions of First Aid in the marine environment and recent, relevant boating experience is essential.

First Aid Instructor course dates can be downloaded from the RYA website.

13.7 SEA SURVIVAL INSTRUCTOR

The four-day Sea Survival Instructor course allows plenty of time for candidates to get to grips with both the classroom delivery and running the swimming-pool session.

Applicants must be an RYA Yachtmaster Instructor or Advanced Powerboat Instructor and hold the RYA Sea Survival course completion certificate.

The Instructor course is organised centrally by the RYA. It is always heavily subscribed. If you are interested in attending, please send your CV to training@rya.org.uk.

13.8 OCEAN INSTRUCTOR

To become an Ocean Instructor you must hold an RYA Yachtmaster Ocean Certificate of Competence, be either a Shorebased (Navigation) Instructor or RYA Yachtmaster Instructor, and apply in writing to RYA Training. In addition, those wishing to run the RYA Yachtmaster Ocean Shorebased course must hold the RYA Yachtmaster Ocean Certificate of Competence.

13.9 TEACHING THE NAVIGATION COURSES

The purpose of the Shorebased Navigation courses is to provide an opportunity for would-be skippers and crew to learn about the principles of such subjects as navigation and meteorology.

ESSENTIAL NAVIGATION AND SAFETY

This entry-level course introduces navigation and safety awareness for new or inexperienced skippers and crew. It is a two-day classroom course, or can be taken as an online course.

DAY SKIPPER

This is a comprehensive introduction to cruising for inexperienced skippers. The theory topics covered are aimed at a taking a boat out in familiar waters by day. The course is taught over 40 hours with two exam papers. It can be covered as a series of short sessions, as an intensive week-long course, or by distance learning. A five-day intensive course is possible for Day Skipper.

COASTAL SKIPPER/RYA YACHTMASTER OFFSHORE

A more advanced course in navigation and meteorology. It is suitable for students who already have the knowledge from the Day Skipper Theory course, or have a background of cruising or offshore racing. The course is definitely not suitable for beginners. It is aimed at those wishing to navigate coastal and offshore passages.

The course should involve a minimum of 40 hours' teaching and allow sufficient time for assessment papers. For Coastal Skipper, a minimum of seven days is usually required.

RYA YACHTMASTER OCEAN

A course in astro navigation and worldwide meteorology. A knowledge of terrestrial navigation and basic meteorology up to the standard of the Coastal Skipper/RYA Yachtmaster Offshore Shorebased course is assumed. This course is for those aspiring to blue-water cruise and is ideal for holders of the RYA Yachtmaster Offshore certificate who are preparing for their first ocean passage.

COURSE PLANNING

As an Instructor, you should make out an overall plan of the entire course. The syllabus in the logbook gives the minimum time allocation for each topic, which will assist in the planning.

When planning the course, think in terms of building blocks of knowledge – what must the learner know before this can be taught? At the same time, remember that learning activity is best done in 20-minute chunks. Frequent changes of learning activity – be it individual exercises, work in pairs, or group work – helps to maintain focus and maximise learning. It can also make it more sociable and fun!

It is important that each student has completed all the exercises and assessments satisfactorily. This means that they must all be marked, though with the short exercises this is often best done in the classroom. The RYA exercises are not intended to be the only questions that the students should attempt during the course. Instructors should provide their own problems based on the syllabus to ensure that every student really understands each topic. Preparing these exercises is time consuming and hard work, but this is time well spent as they can be used again.

14 THE ORGANISATION AND CONDUCT OF RYA YACHTMASTER COASTAL AND RYA YACHTMASTER OFFSHORE EXAMS

14.1 INTRODUCTION

The purpose of these notes is to set guidelines for the conduct of exams.

14.2 AUTHORISATION OF EXAMS

UK exams may be booked through an RYA-recognised training centre or online at www.rya.org.uk.

Exams outside the UK must be organised through an RYA training centre recognised for practical cruising courses for the discipline in which the exam is being taken. The overseas exam location must be approved by the RYA.

An individual candidate who applies to a centre may be put in touch with an examiner to make the detailed arrangements for the exam. RYA training centres must use a pool of examiners rather than relying on one or two for all of their exams. Examiners must not examine at training centres in which they are engaged as full-time employees.

14.3 PAYMENT OF EXAM FEE

The exam fee is payable by the candidate to the RYA. Examiners must ensure that the exam report is accompanied by the appropriate cheque, credit or debit card payment. Examiners may not accept any payment from candidates for expenses incurred in connection with an exam. For exams outside the UK where it is agreed prior to the exam an examiner may have travel expenses reimbursed by an RYA-recognised training centre.

14.4 CANDIDATE'S ELIGIBILITY TO TAKE AN EXAM

Before the start of an exam the examiner must verify the candidate's claim to have the specified sea experience. All candidates must complete and sign the exam application form, which includes a statement of qualifying experience. If there is any doubt as to whether or not the necessary seatime has been completed, the examiner should point this out to the candidate and give them the opportunity to withdraw their application. Candidates for RYA Yachtmaster Coastal and RYA Yachtmaster Offshore must hold a radio operator's certificate. In most cases this will be the RYA Short Range Certificate (SRC) in radiotelephony but any higher qualification, such as the Restricted or General Certificate of Competence or for foreign nationals an equivalent certificate issued by their own administration, is acceptable, providing that it is GMDSS compliant. Candidates for RYA Yachtmaster Coastal and RYA Yachtmaster Offshore must hold a current, approved First Aid certificate. A list of First Aid certificates that are approved can be found on the RYA website. If the certificate is not listed as approved your application will be unable to be processed.

14.5 GENERAL STANDARDS TO BE SET BY EXAMINERS

It is important that examiners are above criticism in their general conduct in all their dealings with candidates. Examiners represent both the RYA and the MCA through their RYA Yachtmaster Examiner appointment. In particular, examiners must:

▶ Be punctual in keeping appointments for exams

▶ Set a standard of dress and appearance which is at least as high as that of the candidate

▶ Respect the candidate's or boat owner's wishes on smoking while on board

▶ Be courteous to candidates and crew throughout the exam

▶ Not be seen to criticise the school for which they are examining

▶ Not be seen to be 'touting for business' through the promotion of other RYA schools or the handing out of business cards.

These are, of course, points of which all examiners will be aware. The reason for including this reminder is that a candidate who fails is liable to look for points on which to attack the examiner and the system, so it is important not to provide any ammunition.

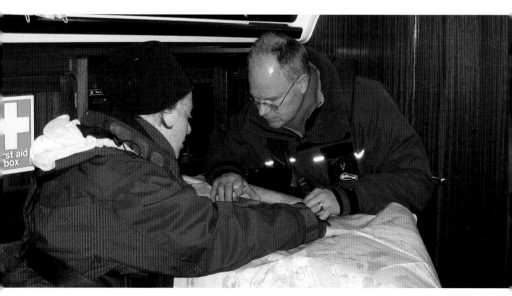

14.6 CONTENT OF THE EXAMINATION

GENERAL

The content of the exam is set by the syllabus in the RYA publication G158 and the headings in the report form. There are two general principles which should be taken as an overall guide:

1 It is the examiner's task to give the candidates the opportunity to show that they are competent skippers.

2 At the end of the exam the candidates should feel, whatever the outcome, that they have had a full, fair, and searching test.

The examiner must remind the candidate that they are there for the purpose of assessment and not to instruct or coach. Candidates who have been through an extended period of training with an RYA school will be used to regular feedback and debriefing and for this reason may expect this of the examiner unless they are briefed appropriately beforehand. Examiners must walk the fine line of being friendly and approachable without becoming overly familiar or relaxed with the candidates. It is easy to get sucked into an engaging conversation while forgetting what you are there to do. The examiner's challenge is to keep the exam focused while allowing the candidates time during the process to relax and catch their breath.

14.7 CANDIDATE NUMBERS AND EXAM DURATION

PRACTICAL EXAMS

For planning purposes, the following times must be used as guidelines:

RYA Yachtmaster Coastal:

▶ One candidate: 6–10 hours
▶ More than one candidate: 4–8 hours per candidate

RYA Yachtmaster Offshore:

▶ One candidate: 8–12 hours
▶ More than one candidate: 5–9 hours per candidate

All exams should include time under way in darkness. It is, however, accepted that this will not be possible in high latitudes in mid-summer – for this reason exams in high latitudes in mid-summer should be avoided where feasible. Examiners must not plan to examine more than two candidates in any 24-hour period. It is important that examiners take a realistic view of their own concentration span as well as that of candidates and should not attempt prolonged exam sessions. No more than four candidates should be examined during any one session (spaced over two days and an evening) as the process becomes repetitive and predictable.

If examining four candidates, the period the examinations must be conducted over is a minimum of two days. This must include sufficient night hours to ensure all candidates conducted some of their examination under way during hours of darkness.

14.8 CONVERSION PRACTICAL EXAMINATIONS

Holders of the RYA Yachtmaster Offshore Sail certificate may take a conversion examination to obtain the RYA Yachtmaster Offshore Power certificate.

EXPERIENCE

At least half the required experience for RYA Yachtmaster Offshore must be in a power vessel such as a motor cruiser:

- ▶ 1,250 miles

- ▶ 25 days

- ▶ Three days as skipper

- ▶ Three passages over 60 miles including
  - one overnight and
  - one as skipper

The exam will take about three hours. The examiner may ask questions or set tasks on any part of the syllabus but will concentrate on those sections which are markedly different in a motor cruiser, e.g. boat handling, passage planning, radar and higher-speed navigation.

RYA Yachtmaster Offshore power candidates may convert to sail. The same rules apply but the exam will be slightly longer.

A similar process is also available for conversion from RYA Yachtmaster Coastal sail to RYA Yachtmaster Coastal power with a minimum of 400 miles' experience on motor cruisers, 12 days living aboard, two days as skipper and 12 night hours (all on board the type of craft for which the conversion exam is being conducted (e.g. from sail to power)).

A specific fee for the conversion exam is revised annually and is available on the RYA website.

14.9 EXERCISE SCENARIOS

In order to carry out a thorough test, examiners may find it convenient to devise exercise scenarios. This may sometimes be a valid and acceptable method but there are a number of pitfalls which must be avoided.

It is important that the examiner is careful to give a full explanation of the scenario, which must be as simple as possible and credible to the candidate. If the examiner fails to do this, the exam degenerates into a role-playing farce.

The scenario must be designed to test a particular skill and the examiner must confine his assessment to the candidate's demonstration of that skill. A candidate will seldom accept failure if the reason is inability to complete an artificial exercise to the examiner's satisfaction. The reason for failure must be expressed in terms of failure to demonstrate a particular skill.

14.10 STRESS MANAGEMENT

The candidate's ability to make sound decisions under pressure is an integral part of the test. The examiner must ensure that the pressure is from the specific circumstances of the situation and not from the examiner personally. The objective is to assess the candidate's competency as a skipper and a seaman, not their ability to pass exams.

Candidates react to the exam situation in a variety of ways and the examiner must make an early assessment of the extent to which exam nerves are going to be a barrier to a fair test. The examiner should, by their personal demeanour, put the candidate at ease and make sure that at no time does the test degenerate into a personality confrontation.

The examiner can unwittingly build up stress in a number of ways. He or she should be particularly careful to avoid, for instance:

▶ Any remark which the candidate might interpret as being gratuitously disparaging

▶ Apparent secretiveness about his intentions during the exam

▶ Prolonged periods of silence

▶ Quick-fire questions

▶ Irrelevant questions when the candidate is trying hard to concentrate on the task in hand.

Stress can be reduced by:

1 Setting a straightforward practical task and giving a genuine 'well done' at the end (assuming it was successful).

2 Taking an interest in the candidate and communicating in a non-confrontational way.

3 A sense of humour – but do not make the candidate the butt of the joke, and do avoid sarcasm.

4 Providing a thorough brief at the beginning of the exam so that both the candidate and crew have a clear understanding of what will be involved in the exam and what the expectation is of each of them.

14.11 USE OF CREW

It is important to make it clear to the candidate and their crew what role the crew is expected to play. Everyone on board must be made aware that the examiner has to test the candidate and any attempt by the crew to prompt the skipper is liable to lose rather than gain points for the candidate. This does not mean that the crew should act dumb – they should play a full part in running the boat but they must not anticipate the  candidate's decisions. The most important part of the exam is the candidate's ability to lead, motivate and communicate, so the examiner must be careful not to erect artificial barriers between skipper and crew. Again, a clear briefing to the skipper and crew prior to the commencement of the exam goes a long way to towards avoiding any confusion.

14.12 SPECIFIC ASPECTS OF PRACTICAL EXAMS

The exam must be set in the context that the candidate is the skipper of the boat. It is important to make it clear that the examiner is there only to observe and assess. The candidate is the skipper at all times with full responsibility for the safety of the boat and crew. The examiner should exercise control over the boat only so far as it is necessary to set up a test and should not take direct control unless he or she feels that it is necessary to prevent damage to the crew or boat.

THE ORGANISATION AND CONDUCT OF OFFSHORE EXAMS

PREPARATION OF BOAT AND CREW

The aim of this section is to test whether the candidate knows what checks on boat and equipment should be carried out and what points should be included in a briefing to a newly joined crew.

PASSAGE PLANNING

The test should show that the candidate understands the passage-planning process. The test may be pre-set so that the candidate arrives for the exam with a passage already planned. Alternatively, the passage-planning ability of the candidate may be done on a purely oral basis by questioning the candidate with a chart and almanac in front of them, allowing you to examine in more or less a 'live environment'. Both methods have their advantages and disadvantages. Whichever method you choose you must be confident by the end of the exam that the candidate has properly demonstrated their understanding of and ability to plan a passage effectively.

BOAT HANDLING (ENTERING AND LEAVING HARBOUR)

The test should, so far as possible, be so arranged that if the candidate is going to get it wrong they can be allowed to do so without causing damage. This avoids any subsequent question as to whether a 'failure' was that of the examiner's nerve rather than the candidate's ability.

PILOTAGE

Whenever possible the candidate should be required to take the boat into confined waters with which they are unfamiliar.

BOAT HANDLING (OPEN WATER)

The test should require the candidate to sail the boat efficiently. This is an area which calls for fine judgement on the part of the examiner, who must distinguish between the ability to set the boat up to win races and the ability to use the sails with an acceptable degree of efficiency.

MAN-OVERBOARD RECOVERY

Every candidate should be required to carry out a man-overboard recovery exercise. Ensure that the candidate is clear whether the engine can be used. This point is at the examiner's discretion. Candidates should be told during the initial briefing to expect a man-overboard task but the actual MOB exercise should be orchestrated to occur without warning. We are looking to see not just whether the candidate can return the boat to the man in the water but in fact whether the candidate can manage crew, vessel and the situation to effect a safe and realistic recovery in a controlled fashion.

NAVIGATION AND CHARTWORK

In general the candidate should be encouraged to navigate as they would normally. If he or she chooses to do no formal chartwork and rely instead on 'by-eye' navigation, the examiner must decide whether or not this is safe.

Chartwork must be tested and in order to do so the examiner may have to impose a scenario which makes chartwork essential for the safe navigation of the boat. Navigation with and without access to electronic position fixing systems should be included. We must know that the candidate is competent both in traditional and electronic navigation techniques and that he or she understands the advantages and disadvantages of both.

DECKWORK AND GENERAL SEAMANSHIP

There are two aspects to be tested: decision making and practical ability to implement decisions. Do not assume that because a candidate regards themselves as a skipper he or she can carry out elementary routine tasks. Occasionally you will encounter a candidate who cannot tie a bowline.

IRPCS

The test should show that the candidate knows the correct lights/shapes for his own boat, can recognise any vessel by special lights or shapes, assess risk of collision and take the correct action in any situation where risk of collision exists. Questions requiring retained knowledge of specific local regulations should not be used. We wish to confirm that the candidate understands and can apply the rules of the road, rather than whether he or she can recite them by number.

METEOROLOGY

The test should include knowledge of what forecasts are available, the interpretation of forecasts and visible phenomena. This section of the exam should be related to passage planning and strategy. It should not be an academic exercise. Candidates <u>must</u> be able to discuss weather in the context of a planned passage and how/if a specific weather scenario will impact their passage over several days.

OVERALL ABILITY AS SKIPPER

All items should be tested within the overall context of the candidate's ability as skipper. The level of difficulty of the test and the standard of expertise required to pass depends on whether the exam is for RYA Yachtmaster Coastal or RYA Yachtmaster Offshore. At RYA Yachtmaster Coastal level the situations should be simple and the candidate should be allowed as much time as they need to complete each task. Crew management should be only that necessary for short passages. At RYA Yachtmaster Offshore level the test situations may be complex and may be set with pressure to complete the situation more quickly. The candidate is expected to be able to organise and manage a crew on passages of up to 48 hours.

CHECKLISTS

A checklist of items to be tested during the exam is set out at the end of this section. There will never be time to cover everything on the list and the purpose is to help to plan a well-balanced exam. Essentially, for a practical exam anything (with the exception of the RYA Yachtmaster Ocean syllabus) that is within the RYA Yachtmaster and Cruising Scheme syllabus is within the scope of the exam. From basic knots through to complex navigational concepts the candidate must have a thorough and testing assessment that covers a broad cross-section of the syllabus.

WEATHER LIMITATIONS

If there is insufficient wind to make a fair assessment of the candidate's sailing ability the examiner and candidate should arrange a mutually convenient date for a retest. There is no additional fee payable by the candidate or to the examiner.

Adverse weather (strong winds or poor visibility) is an integral part of the exam process. It is reasonable for the examiner to fail a candidate who declines to go out in conditions under which a candidate capable of passing the exam could safely put to sea. There will be occasions on which it is unsafe to carry out a test, in which case it will be necessary to arrange another date for the exam.

PASS/FAIL RECOMMENDATION

In deciding whether or not a candidate should pass or fail, a broad view of overall performance should be taken. No candidate is perfect and the examiner must therefore balance strengths and weaknesses when coming to a pass/fail decision. In making this decision the examiner must heavily mark down any indication of unsafe practice, lack of knowledge or poor application of IRPCS. Be careful not to try and form your view too early in the exam. Take notes to ensure that you capture all relevant aspects of the candidate's performance.

Post-exam Debrief

At the end of every exam the examiner should carry out a debriefing session with the candidate. The examiner should stress that he or she is stating his personal view of how the exam went and that the final pass/fail decision rests with the RYA Yachtmaster Qualification Panel (although in practice it is most unusual for an examiner's recommendation to be reversed).

If the candidate is being recommended for a certificate the debrief can be relatively short. However, we must recognise that even a successful candidate will be eager to know exactly how well he or she did. Ensure you provide enough feedback (both positive as well as constructive criticism) that the candidate goes away satisfied that they are clear on any areas that may benefit from further practice.

If the candidate is not to be recommended for a pass, the purpose of the debrief is to make the process of failure as kind and as positive as possible. Praise any good points which emerged during the test but do not gloss over the bad points, which should be treated in the vein 'What you might do to improve this so that you pass next time is...'. It is absolutely essential that the debrief is honest and open, but most importantly that the candidate leaves with a clear understanding of what they must work on prior to another attempt at the exam. The debrief should mirror what is written in the exam report.

EXAM REPORTS

The exam report must be completed and forwarded to the RYA at the earliest possible opportunity, not more than five working days after the exam. The exam report is in two sections: a factual report on the candidate's ability (the back of the exam report) and a recommendation on how to remedy any deficiencies (the front of the exam report – which must be completed for any candidates who will not be recommended as a pass).

Those who fail are sent a copy of the exam report so it is important that the debrief and exam report are not contradictory. Language in the report should be clear and unambiguous, backing up the debrief conversation. At the same time, the language used should be such that it will be viewed as constructive feedback rather than an indictment of a disastrous exam attempt.

The RYA offers a fast-track service for a speedy turnaround of certificate. A fee is chargeable.

PARTIAL RE-EXAMINATION

A candidate who fails in a single section of the exam and is good in all other sections may be retested by the same examiner within a period of six weeks. In such cases an additional fee, as laid down by the RYA, is to be charged. The retest procedure is intended for candidates who fail one of the 'memory test' subjects, but examiners may use their discretion in asking candidates to take a retest in any subject, providing it does not require you to put to sea. The exam report should not be forwarded until the re-examination has been completed.

It is important that the partial resit is used only at the discretion of the examiner. For this reason it is essential that partial resits are only mentioned after an exam and when an examiner can reasonably make themselves available to conduct the exam. Mentioning it prior to the exam runs the risk of encouraging any 'failed' candidate to begin negotiating for a partial reassessment.

BARRIERS TO EXAMINATION

An examiner must not examine a candidate who is a personal friend, whom they have taught, or previously failed in an examination. They must also not examine students from a centre at which the examiner is a full-time employee.

Examiners must examine only in boats of a type of which they have experience and which they would themselves be confident to skipper.

14.13 RYA YACHTMASTER COASTAL/RYA YACHTMASTER OFFSHORE EXAMINATION CHECKLIST

PRIOR TO GOING TO SEA

Preparation of Boat and Crew

Safety brief	Crew brief
Stowage on deck/below	Watch-keeping plan
Boat checks	Sail selection
Engine checks	

Passage Planning

Selection of destination	Selection of charts (correction)
Tidal calculations	Selection of route – entering waypoints
Tidal-stream prediction	Prediction of CTS and ETA

ENTERING/LEAVING HARBOUR

Boat Handling
General

► Use of warps

► Boat control under sail

► Boat control under power

► Briefing and use of crew

Specific

Berthing:

▶ Alongside

▶ Piles

▶ Buoy under sail

▶ Buoy under power

▶ Anchor under sail

▶ Anchor under power

Unberthing:

▶ Alongside

▶ Piles

▶ Buoy under sail

▶ Buoy under power

▶ Anchor under sail

▶ Anchor under power

Pilotage

Pilotage plan

Crew briefing and organisation

Control of boat

Execution of plan

AT SEA

Seamanship and Boat Handling

Helmsmanship

Sail trim

Sail selection

Man-overboard recovery

Situational awareness

Navigation and Chartwork

Position fixing – visual

Position fixing – RNAs

Use of GPS and/or plotter

Use of echo sounder

Course shaping

Working up EP

Keeping the log

Navigation in restricted visibility

Secondary means of position fixing

Radar – position fixing

Knowledge of buoyage and chart symbols

Navigational strategy

Deckwork and General Seamanship

Safety of crew – use of harnesses	Crew motivation and leadership
Sail changing	Preparations for heavy weather
Chafe prevention	Conduct in restricted visibility
Lookout	Periodic engine checks

SPECIFIC SUBJECTS

IRPCS

Theoretical knowledge

Practical application

Uses and limitations of AIS

Basic radar use for collision avoidance

Meteorology

Knowledge of forecasts available

Interpretation and application of forecasts

Characteristics of highs and lows

Use of barometer and visual signs

14.14 INTERNATIONAL CERTIFICATE OF COMPETENCE

The ICC is required by some European countries for certain categories of pleasure boat. See the RYA website for further information about providing evidence of competence abroad.

An ICC can be obtained from the RYA by completing an application form and either:

1 Sending a copy of an RYA practical course completion certificate relevant to the category of ICC for which they are applying (see the RYA website for details of categories).

2 Re-applying on expiry of a Helmsman's Overseas Certificate of Competence (predecessor to the ICC).

3 Passing a practical and oral test at a test centre (direct assessment)

The issue of the ICC is free to RYA members. Non-members are charged a fee.

TEST CENTRES

Only RYA-recognised practical training centres or affiliated clubs with qualified testers may be used as test centres. Centres and clubs may only offer tests for the disciplines for which their testers are qualified.

TESTERS

Testers can be RYA Yachtmaster Instructors, Cruising Instructors or RYA Yachtmasters who have attended a tester training course.

CONDUCT OF TESTS

The syllabus and tasks required for the practical test are given on the application form available from the RYA.

Oral

The RYA can provide test centres with sample questions.

Practical

The purpose of the practical test is to give every candidate the opportunity to show that they are capable of skippering a boat without endangering or damaging other people, boats or the marine environment. Some coaching is permitted during the test to help the candidate achieve the required standard. The candidate can reasonably expect politeness and good humour from the person carrying out the test.

The biggest barrier to a successful test is the candidate's nerves. This can be overcome by the following:

▶ Having a friendly and relaxed manner yourself.

▶ Getting the candidate involved in an activity as quickly as possible (without putting pressure on them).

▶ If the candidate has carried out a manoeuvre well, then say so.

▶ Not being inscrutable. Talk to the candidate and the rest of the crew. The existence of any test implies that there must be people who will not be up to standard. The tester's most difficult job is to break the bad news as gently as possible.

This can be made easier by:

▶ Making sure the candidate knows that their overall performance has been below standard. In many cases it will be obvious because of the failure to complete an exercise. Try to set practical tests which can be failed without requiring the tester to stop the exercise or take over control.

▶ Debriefing constructively. Praise what was done well. Suggest ways of improving what was done badly rather than simply stating that it was below an acceptable standard.

▶ If possible, organise a retest of the tasks which were not achieved. A deferment is always more palatable than a straight fail.